Also by Jeff Foster

Life Without a Centre
Beyond Awakening
The Revelation of Oneness

AN EXTRAORDINARY ABSENCE

Liberation in the Midst of
a Very Ordinary Life

JEFF FOSTER

NON-DUALITY PRESS

ACKNOWLEDGEMENTS

Deep gratitude to Nathan Gill
Special thanks to Philip Pegler

With love to:
Adam, Amy, Barry, Joan, John, Josh, Julian, Jeannine,
Kriben, Lynda, Mandi, Menno, Mike,
Nic, Pamela, Sid, Tijn, Wendy,
and everyone else!

AN EXTRAORDINARY ABSENCE

First edition published September 2009 by NON-DUALITY PRESS
© Jeff Foster 2009
© Non-Duality Press 2009
Cover photograph by Nic Oestreicher
nhoestreicher@googlemail.com.
Author photograph by Fleur van der Minne.

Typeset in Plantin & Stone Informal
Non-Duality Press | PO Box 2228 | Salisbury | SP2 2GZ
United Kingdom

ISBN: 978-0-9563091-0-5

www.non-dualitypress.com

If you coul d get rid of yourself just once,
The secret of secrets would open to you.
The face of the Unknown, hidden beyond the universe,
Would appear on the mirror of your perception.

- Rumi

Love says "I am everything".
Wisdom says "I am nothing".
Between the two, my life flows.

- Nisargadatta Maharaj

Foreword

Jeff Foster and I met recently in Brighton for a lengthy dialogue about the nondual perspective. Along the way we got sidetracked by our shared passion for magic tricks. One of the card illusions which Jeff shared with me during our conversation was called 'Deep Astonishment'. And when Jeff asked me to write the foreword to his new book, that name popped up, which I thought apt for what I wanted to share about the book and the deepest implication of it all; and that is the deepest astonishment, which, as I will attempt to show, is about the deepest illusion.

If you do an internet search for nondual teachers, you will be quite surprised by the sheer number of 'awakened ones' out there, many of them performing extremely delicate feats of sleight of speech to proclaim their enlightenment. But this is precisely what Jeff's book is about: that there is no one who can be enlightened. And this is where the sleight of speech comes in, similar to the 'mind-reader' who proclaims he is not a psychic but has simply developed acute skills of psychological observation to give the impression of paranormal abilities. In fact, neither is true, and the 'mind-reader' is simply engaging in a double deception through linguistic manipulation and artful theatre.

Much of the current nondual scene is similarly engaged in layered deceptions, and I would suggest that part of this deception arises from the deepest self-deception: "I have disappeared and there is only That, and I am now liberated". Now, this verbal formulation is tricky. It could possibly be an accurate utterance through the persona of one where the unreality of the person has been apperceived, or it could be a formulaic expression by someone who is intentionally creating an illusion, or is simply deluded. These are harsh words and I make no apology for them, because it's time we moved beyond appearances to see that it's all appearance. Everything. My liberation, or lack of it, my evolutionary enlightenment, or lack of it, and my wonderful card tricks. And that's the deepest astonishment.

And this brings me to Jeff's book. There are sections that speak the conventional language of nonduality, and this can best be described as expression that grapples with a dualistic tool to convey that which is nondualistic. There is a certain linguistic tension when words emanate from a Mystery which can never be revealed. Apparent sense collapses into non-sense, and paradox announces itself as the vehicle of a Truth which cannot be known. All of this can be found in Jeff's writings, but this book extends the boundaries of the genre, where the impersonal descriptive is counterpointed by personal confessional passages. Here, Jeff lets the reader see Jeff the character; the everyday guy on the block who is just like you and me in every way. But here's the difficult part to articulate: this character, through the deepest astonishment of seeing that it is all just an illusion, collapses into a Mystery where the world, in all its myriad appearances, is both very ordinary and extraordinary. And the ordinary would be you and I and Jeff. And the extraordinary would be the profound absence of all that we take to be real.

Kriben Pillay
Associate Professor, The Leadership Centre
University of KwaZulu-Natal
May 2009

Contents

Introduction

At the very heart of this book is the simple, direct and timeless message of *nonduality*. The word *nonduality* is often used nowadays to describe the ancient Indian *Advaitic* tradition of spirituality. It simply means *not two* and is indicating the essential Oneness of life. There is only one reality–Oneness is all there is and we are included.

The book has a deeply caring quality that cannot easily be framed in words. The writing sounds a quiet note of authority that is compelling and commands respect. Nevertheless, everyone is free to listen or walk away, and Jeff Foster is unequivocal about this. When you are talking about the subject of nonduality, you are always talking about something that cannot be spoken of, he says. It is a truth that cannot be told–it is a plunge into the mystery.

This is certainly a liberating message to be explored with an open mind! We do not need to move elsewhere in order to find truth, for it is always present in the clear immediacy of our own direct experience. Truth is always made manifest in the form of whatever is happening moment by moment. It is just this... and this–nothing else. The problem is we are always moving away from what is before us–this is never enough. Neither do we need the endless and exhausting search to attain spiritual freedom–it is already profoundly present within the natural spaciousness of our true being. Yet we do need to recognise and honour this inherent freedom in order to make it our own.

What is so rare and remarkable about this book is the particularly clear way in which Jeff leads us carefully step by step to directly experience for ourselves what is true. We need to begin where we are, and he sweetly implores us to meet every experience freshly with new eyes. In all sorts of original and creative ways, he asks us repeatedly to meet life head-on without preconceived ideas – and then report what we find.

If only such gentle courtesy was always enough to help us see clearly! When you meet Jeff Foster, you encounter someone who is refreshingly natural. He is quite disarming, but he also has an incisive quality of fierce candour, which cuts through evasion and hypocrisy. Life is just too short and precious to waste time in endless disputes about the nature of enlightenment or the rights and wrongs of authentic spiritual practice – and what exactly constitutes the purest non-dual teaching method. He knows full well from his own profound experience that sometimes what is required above all is a courageous resolve to go the whole way – to proceed down the 'road less travelled' come what may – until our doubts are finally resolved.

We can never do so with our own strength, yet there is no cause for concern, for the strength that we need will always be provided from the universe to which we naturally belong. Love comes to everyone in the end – and it is a love with no name, which we finally understand has never been absent.

There are no neat formulae or glib answers. This beautiful direct teaching about the Oneness of life is unbelievably simple and straightforward, but it is also open to misunderstanding. There are numerous pitfalls for the unwary, as is made plain in these pages. A sure guide is sometimes needed – and in Jeff Foster you need not be disappointed. Nevertheless, he insists he is not a teacher; the books and meetings are but a sharing with friends:

I have no interest in what the world calls me. And for the sheer joy of it, I'll share this message until I don't. People will listen, or they will walk away, and it's fine either way.

And right now, as I sip my cup of tea, and watch the seagulls on Brighton Pier, none of it matters in the slightest. I laugh at the idea that I'm a teacher or guru. I'm nothing. The tea and the seagulls are everything. My nothing is the world's everything, and it all ends here, in absolute simplicity, and there is only love for all of it.

Here is a young author, with a wisdom and maturity beyond his years, sharing with his readers a precious secret, which is all too often missed. At the heart of this poetic message is the profound insight that liberation is never far away—it is always present in the midst of so-called ordinary, everyday life. Freedom is everywhere and in everything—there is no division between sacred and secular. It is nothing special and yet... it is somehow there equally in joy and wonder as well as in unutterable sorrow and grievous pain. This is beyond comprehension. It keeps one humble and there are no adequate words for what may be realised.

This is not a book to lightly read and put aside. It is a thoughtful and compassionate book to stick with and then dip into again and again—especially if you do not understand some of what it hints at in the beginning. The writing is in turn reflective, comic and challenging with a music all of its own. The gentle harmony gets under your skin and into your very bones, working its insistent magic. This is truly the alchemy of transformation.

You see, this is not only about the words—it is more about the *resonance* of those words. Charged with conviction, such words have the power to call forth a very special quality from deep within us. It is a kind of sweet, nostalgic fragrance—the recognition of something familiar we already know but cannot articulate. It is truth, love and beauty. These are all inspiring terms that point to different aspects of the essential underlying reality, which cannot be named but only pointed to.

The end of the spiritual search is the clear recognition of 'an extraordinary absence'. It is the complete absence of separation, together with the wondrous discovery of the true presence of the entire world in a love and intimacy beyond anything we have ever known.

Philip Pegler
Midhurst, England
June 2009

AN
EXTRAORDINARY
ABSENCE

A New Beginning

This book is a love letter from Silence to Silence.

The words emerge from Silence and return to it.

Words are merely ripples on the surface of the vast Ocean of Being.

They dance and play and sing their song, and then dive back into that infinite expanse of aliveness.

Read the words and leave them behind.

Read the words and then throw this book away.

Burn it.

All words can do is point. They are pointers. Signposts.

They cannot touch Life, they cannot capture it, but perhaps, just perhaps, they can point to it.

Perhaps, just perhaps, they can communicate something of the taste of it, something of the fragrance of it.

These words in this book are pointing to something very simple.

To Life as it unfolds.
To the simple and obvious present appearance of everything.
To present sights, sounds and smells.
To the aliveness that is behind everything, that fuels everything, that transcends everything, that *is* everything.

And beyond even that:

To the absence of a separate, solid person.
To a vast openness which holds everything and is not separate from everything.
To the extraordinary absence at the heart of life which finally reveals itself as a perfect presence.

The seeming paradox at the heart of creation:

Absence is presence.
Emptiness is form.
Awareness is not separate from its content.

And when absence and presence meet each other and implode,
when emptiness and form become each other and disappear,
when the one who sees collapses into what is seen,
when subject and object become mad, mad lovers and vanish into thin air,
what remains?

When all the concepts in the world
are seen to be just concepts,
when thought falls back into its natural rhythm,
when the futile seeking of the 'monkey mind' comes to rest at last,
what is there?

Beyond awakening, beyond enlightenment, beyond the real and the unreal,
beyond existence and non-existence, beyond *what is* and *what is not*,
beyond self and no-self, beyond duality and nonduality,
beyond life and death,
beyond all beyonds, what shines?

What gave life to you, what brought you out of itself, aeons ago, so that it could know itself? So that it could touch, taste, feel, see itself?

What holds you, loves you, embraces you, always, the way a mother embraces her newborn baby?

What has always been calling you back to itself, right from the very beginning?

This.

Only *this.*

Always *this.*

Forever *this.*

I respectfully ask that you forget everything you know, everything you've been taught, everything you've ever read about spiritual awakening, nonduality, Advaita, Oneness, and enlightenment, and consider a new possibility: the possibility of liberation, right here in the midst of this seemingly ordinary life. The possibility of absolute freedom, right where you are.

And now, let's begin again.

1

THE WAVE AND THE OCEAN

And, for no reason,
I start skipping like a child.
And, for no reason, I turn into a leaf
That is carried so high
I kiss the sun's mouth
And dissolve.

- Hafiz

Out Beyond Ideas

I am not a teacher. I don't have anything that you don't. I am not special in any way. I mean that.

If we had to give a name to what this is, we could call it a *sharing*. A sharing, in friendship and openness, of something that's already known, something that's already intimately known. Really, I don't need to tell you a single thing about this.

You've always known this. I'm just here to remind you.

Sometimes people talk about a recognition or a resonance that can happen when you read or listen to words that emanate from Clarity. This resonance is completely beyond the thinking mind, beyond the intellect, beyond our understanding. It is this resonance that goes right to the heart of what is being communicated in this book.

In that resonance there is always the possibility of something else shining through. That's really what all these words are trying to point to: an illumination that's beyond understanding. A recognition that's beyond thought. An opening up into something more extraordinary–and more ordinary–than the mind could ever hope to grasp.

* * *

When we talk about nonduality we often have to resort to using metaphors and paradoxes, because we're trying to point to something that is living and whole using words that fragment and divide. It's like trying to catch water in a fishing net. Impossible.

This book is full of such paradoxes and contradictions. And so the mind that's trying to *understand* all of these words intellectually is going to get very confused. The mind so desperately wants to understand, because if it can understand it can possess and if it can possess it can control. It wants to be the master. It has spent the past few million years being the master, and it's not going to give up easily!

Don't try to *understand* anything in this book, but be open to the possibility that an illumination can occur. Just let the words wash over you. Sunbathe in their presence. If you find some of the concepts in this book challenging, that's because they are. They are going to challenge every single idea you have about spirituality and life and the world and yourself. You may even find some of the words quite threatening to your sense of self, to your ideas about who you are, to your notions of truth.

Be open to this other possibility. And know that the one who wrote this book is the one who is reading it. If anything in this book sounds harsh or cruel or uncaring, that is not the intention. The intention is not to shock or upset but to share the possibility of absolute, unconditional love.

In your dream, this book has appeared out of nowhere, in order to remind you of what you already know.

* * *

It's not just the words in this book that are attempting

to communicate this message. It's not just these words that are trying to express the inexpressible. Everything is doing it. Literally everything around you is already expressing liberation, perfectly. It's in the smells, the sounds, the traffic going by, movement happening: everything is *expressing* this, and everything is an *expression* of this. It's everywhere, and we just can't see it. That's the cosmic joke.

So don't get too attached to the words in this book. They are just a small part of the dance of life. They are merely ripples on the surface of Being.

If you are reading in a spirit of openness, with an open mind and an open heart, if you are ready to put aside everything you know, if you are open to another possibility, a possibility that seems to go against so much of what we've been conditioned to believe, then perhaps something in what's being shared here will resonate. Perhaps something will be recognised, perhaps something will be seen, perhaps something will fall away; if there's an opening, that is.

And of course, if you're reading this book with a closed mind and a closed heart, then it might all just leave you feeling frustrated and disappointed. You might get so attached to the words that you miss what the words are pointing to. If that's the case, I'd suggest putting the book aside and coming back to it later, if and when there is an opening.

* * *

I should warn you now: *this is not a self-help book*. It isn't about quick fixes. It's not about solving all of your problems. It hasn't been written in order to make you feel better about your imaginary self.

This book is about a *seeing*–a word which seems to encapsulate everything that is being communicated here. Seeing that your problems were never yours in the first place. Seeing that it was never your life to fix. That you were never for one moment separate from Life.

That there is only *this*–here and now–and that it's already complete, and needs no improvement. That what you were always longing for is already staring you in the face, and doesn't look anything like you expected it to.

This is all very good news, you know. As Jesus said, you have to lose your life to save it. Die before you die, said the Prophet Muhammad, and there is no death. When the seeker is no more, there is only love.

If there is a readiness to listen, an openness and a willingness to let go, then welcome to this 'quiet revolution in spirituality'.

The Search For Home

Let's get right to the root of it:

This never seems to be enough.

What's happening right now, the present moment, *this*, never seems to be enough. In a million different ways, we spend our lives seeking, searching, wanting.

Looking for something more.
Something else.
Something other than what's happening.
Something—in the future—that will satisfy us, complete us, save us.
Looking for the answers. Driving ourselves mad with the questions.

We never seem to be able to just come to rest here, to fully relax into what's happening. There is a constant pull into a future moment when things will be better. And with our attention so fixed on the future—and its reflection, the past—what's presently happening gets reduced to a means to an end, just one moment in a series of many. We hope that future moments will be better than this one. We just never seem to be content with *this*.

This is what I call the search. This is what I call seeking. We are all seekers. We are all looking for something.

And the search manifests itself in a million different ways. In the so-called material world there's the search for money, happiness, status, better and more fulfilling relationships, a stronger sense of self. More things. More security. In the material world it's very important to know who you are. To fulfil your destiny. To make your life work. To achieve your goals, your ambitions. To succeed. It's the search to be someone in the world. To make something of your life before you die.

And so often the so-called material world doesn't satisfy us. And so we might turn to spiritual teachings. And now the goal is no longer a million pounds in the bank account, or a faster car, or a more fulfilling marriage. Now the goal is awakening. Now the goal is enlightenment. Now, instead of the new car, we want the altered state of consciousness. Instead of the new relationship we want permanent bliss. Instead of worldly success we want enlightenment, we want to lose something called an ego, we want to transcend something called the mind.

Material seeking, spiritual seeking, it's all seeking. Whether it's the search for material wealth or spiritual enlightenment, it's the same seeking, the same movement of thought. It's a movement into a non-existent future.

It's the search for something in the future, for *me*.

Yes, what goes right to the root of all this seeking, is the '*me*'.

We want the million pounds in the bank account for *me*, and we want the spiritual enlightenment for *me*. *Me, me, me!*

At the root of all the seeking of a lifetime is the sense

that there is an individual here, a separate me, a separate self, a separate person.

It's the sense of being an entity separate from life itself, separate from *this*. Separate from others, separate from the world. Separate from the Source.

At the root of all the seeking of a lifetime is a sense of not being whole. Of being incomplete. Fragmented. Lost. Alienated. Homesick.

For the separate individual, that sense of lack seems to seep into every part of life. *Never enough, never enough,* that is the mantra of the separate self. And this sense of lack is not merely an intellectual thing. It's not just a belief. It's a deeply felt sense of not being at home, a sense which infuses all experience.

Once we were home, and now we are not. As separate individuals, we live haunted by the vague memory of an intimacy that we cannot name.

It's like when you were a very young child and your mother left you alone in the room. You didn't know where she'd gone and you were suddenly overcome by a longing, a homesickness, that you could not explain, but which seemed to go right to the very core of who or what you were.

This longing goes right to the heart of what it means to be a separate person.

And yet, as we shall see, it's not mother that we really want; she is just a symbol of something far greater. We all long to return home, back to the Source, back to the

Ocean. Back to what we were before all of this happened.

*   *   *

And so the moment you have separation, you also have a *longing*. It's the longing to end the separation. To heal the divide. To end the sense of contraction and expand back into the vastness.

It's the wave longing to collapse back into the ocean. But of course, what the wave cannot see is that there never was a wave separate from the ocean. The wave was always a perfect manifestation of the ocean. It was always one hundred percent water. It was always soaking wet. Drenched in Being.

You have never been separate from the ocean. You have never been separate from the whole. That was the dream of separation. And the search of a lifetime was always the search for home.

But of course, it was never recognised as that. The longing for home always manifested as the desire for a new car, for more money, for that man or woman. The longing played itself out on a very worldly level, though what you always secretly longed for was the *loss* of your world and a plunge into Life itself.

The Possibility of Liberation

What is being shared in this book is the possibility that the search for home is in vain, because you never left home in the first place. You've only ever been home.

What we'll be sharing in the following pages is the possibility that the seeking of a lifetime, this incessant and exhausting search for something more, something 'out there', something in the future for 'me', can fall away.

The seeking can completely fall away.

And along with it, the sense of being a separate person can fall away too. When the seeking goes, so does the sense of being a separate seeker.

And what can be revealed in the absence of that seeking – well, it's absolutely beyond words.

What can be revealed in that falling away is... liberation.

Liberation, right in the midst of life.

Liberation, right where you are.

And to a mind that's been hooked on its spiritual teachings, beliefs, practices, ideologies, well the simplicity of what is revealed in that falling-away is shocking. It's simply shocking. Stunning in fact.

It's nothing like you thought it would be.

My goodness, we have so many ideas of what liberation is! But right now, what else could they be but thoughts, concepts, memories, carried over from the past? Our ideas about liberation are always second-hand.

But the beauty of *this* is that it cannot be contained by any of those ideas and concepts. It's too alive for that, too present for that.

This is the death of the separate individual, the death of the seeker, and a plunge into something far more mysterious.

Hide and Seek

What appears to be happening here is that someone – me – has written a book on something called nonduality, which someone else – you – is reading right now. This is the dream.

What's actually happening here – and not just here but everywhere else of course – is quite extraordinary. What's happening here is *Oneness meeting itself.* Seeing itself in a million different forms and delighting in that.

Right now, Oneness appears as *this*. It appears as a body sitting on a chair, holding a book. And it appears as the floor, the walls, the heart beating, breathing happening, colours, smells, sounds and everything else that's going on right now.

Oneness appears as everything that's presently happening, absolutely everything. Well of course it does. It *is* everything.

This extraordinary aliveness is staring us in the face, and it always has been. So how come we don't see it all the time? It's so obvious when it is recognised, and yet until then, it appears to be hidden. There appears to be a game of hide and seek going on!

Yes, from one perspective it appears to be incredibly well hidden. So well hidden, in fact, that for a lifetime it has been appearing as everything, quite literally everything, and yet we still can't see it.

And, of course, because it's everything, quite literally everything, nothing is really hidden at all.

If you were going to hide, but wanted to make sure that you were found, the best thing to do would be to disguise yourself as everything that is.

If you wanted to make something completely obvious, wouldn't you make sure that it was everything?

* * *

None of this needs to be understood.

If you could understand this, you would just be a person who had collected some concepts about nonduality. You would just be a person with some *ideas* about what this is.

It's not about understanding, it's about a falling. A falling into the awesome mystery that is life itself. A falling into the not-knowing.

And in that falling, the seeker is no more.

The Offering

In the dream of separation, you are an individual with choice and free will. In the dream, you apparently chose to start reading this book. You chose to go to the bookshop, or borrow the book from a friend, and then today you chose to pick up the book and sit down and start reading. And you're choosing to sit on the chair in a certain way now, and you're choosing to move your eyes across the pages, and you're choosing to believe me or not, to like what I'm saying or not, to be bored or excited by the words, or not. In the dream, you're certainly doing a lot of choosing!

In the dream you chose your way towards this.
In the dream you made all of this happen.
In the dream you can take credit for all of this.
In the dream you appear to be a *creator*.

In the falling away of the story of choice, the story that you're a separate, solid person at the centre of your life, the story that you are doing everything, that you created all of this, you really have no way of knowing how any of this came to be. In the falling away of choice, you have no way of knowing how you got here. How any of this happened.

And then, like a newborn baby, you open your eyes, and you find *this*. In the falling-away of the individual, you're seeing this for the first time. And you look down and you find yourself perched on a chair. And there's the sense that the chair doesn't have to be there, but it is anyway.

25

And there is only gratitude for it all.

You look down, and my goodness there's a chair there, offering itself, supporting you unconditionally, asking nothing of you. What grace.

The chair doesn't care who you are. Who you *think* you are. It doesn't care what you've done or haven't done. It doesn't care what you've achieved or haven't achieved, what you believe or don't believe. It doesn't care if you're a success or a failure, if you've reached your goals or not. It doesn't care whether or not you think you're enlightened. It doesn't care what you look like, what clothes you are wearing. It doesn't care whether you're sick or healthy, whether you're a Buddhist or a Jew or a Christian, whether you are young or old, whether you understand or don't understand. It only offers itself, unconditionally.

This message isn't complicated. It's there in something as simple and commonplace as a chair.

And not just the chair, but all things: all things offer themselves unconditionally.

The secret is this:

Life is not really life at all. It is an offering.

And right now it offers *this*. It offers the present moment. It offers everything that's happening here. It offers this presence, this aliveness. It offers an apparent world of sights and sounds and smells, even though there is nobody there at the centre of it all. Even though, if truth be told, there is no world at all. And yet, there is *this*.

And with the innocent eyes of a child, you are always seeing it for the first time. Words don't even begin to capture it.

To the mind, all of this is madness! The mind says "well of course there's a chair there! I put it there! I made this happen!" The mind could never begin to grasp the wonder of *what is*. Never mind, it doesn't need to. Wonder carries on being wonder even if it goes unrecognised and unappreciated.

* * *

And it goes deeper: you look down and you see clothes on your body, protecting you, keeping you warm or keeping you cool or keeping the sun off you.

And breathing is happening. In and out, in and out, effortlessly. Again, asking nothing of you. And even in deep dreamless sleep, when you aren't even there to know it, breathing is happening. Breathing even happens in the absence of you! You don't even have to be there, and yet the offering just goes on.

And the heart's beating, pumping blood around the body, asking nothing of you. It's just offering itself freely. One day it won't be. One day the heart won't be beating anymore, *but it is now*. One day breathing won't happen anymore, *but it's happening now*. You're not guaranteed anything, you're not guaranteed another day, another hour, another moment. And yet you get all of this. For free.

Sensations in the body, and sounds, and the cool breeze. And even thoughts coming out of nowhere and dissolving back into nothingness. You get all of that as well, for free. This is grace. This is Oneness. And it doesn't look anything like you thought it would. Who would have thought that liberation, or whatever you want to call this, would be so simple and so obvious? That it would be a simple, clear seeing of what is? That it would be life, as it is, seen in clarity?

And of course, the mind will reject this message. You see, this is the end of its story of control. The end of its future. The end of its seeking. To the mind, this is a bit like *death*. And so the mind goes "no, this cannot be it, this is too ordinary! I expected so much more! I wanted so much more than just... sitting on a chair!"

The mind says this is too *ordinary*.

But you see, it was always the search for the extraordinary that made this ordinary. It was always the search for something *out there* that made this so ordinary and dull. And then we got so bored with *this* that we wanted *that*! We got so bored with *this* that we wanted the awakening *from* this!

The spiritual search was always rooted in a rejection of the present. The search of a lifetime was always a movement away from what is.

But in the falling away of the search for the extraordinary, *this* is no longer ordinary. In the falling away of the seeking – and along with it, the seeker – you have no way of calling this 'ordinary' any longer. The opposites collapse into each other, and what you are left with, you have no way of putting into words.

Look at a newborn baby or very young child: there is a sense of wonder there, a sense of amazement at life *as it is*. As adults, we seem to move so far away from that childlike innocence and simplicity. We become so heavy, so lost in our seeking, in our search to be someone in the world, in our drive to succeed, in our desire to make everything perfect. And it's all so exhausting.

Underneath all of the seeking, we're still just newborn babies. We're still seeing the world for the first time. We just got a little lost in the game of *becoming*, that's all.

Rearranging the Furniture

As the mind tries to process all of this information, one of its responses might be:

If seeking is the problem, how do I give it up?

And with that, you see, we are right back into the seeking game. We begin to seek the end of seeking, which is more seeking than ever.

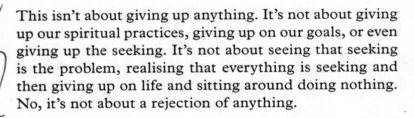This isn't about giving up anything. It's not about giving up our spiritual practices, giving up on our goals, or even giving up the seeking. It's not about seeing that seeking is the problem, realising that everything is seeking and then giving up on life and sitting around doing nothing. No, it's not about a rejection of anything.

You see, in the dream, nothing actually has to change. This is why this book is not like any other book on spirituality. So many spiritual books are about changing your life. Changing your attitude, changing your behaviours, changing your thoughts. Rearranging the furniture in the Hotel Room of Life to make it a more comfortable place to stay. This book will not teach you how to rearrange the furniture. But of course if you want a more comfortable room, by all means rearrange the furniture!

What I'm suggesting is that 'your life' is already *perfect the way it is*, even if that is not yet recognised.

Imagine you're asleep at night, and you're having a dream. And in the dream, all sorts of things happen. Whilst you're having the dream, it all seems so real. And then suddenly you wake up, and you realise that everything that just happened didn't actually happen at all.

Now, nothing in that dream has to change. You don't wake up in the morning and try to change the dream, do you? The seeing of the dream as a dream is enough. In the seeing of the dream as a dream, the dreamer is no more, and nothing that happened in that dream can touch you anymore.

It's the same as when you're watching a movie. You're not sitting in the cinema trying to change or manipulate the movie. You're just watching. And in fact, in the watching, there is no longer a separation between the one who watches and the movie that is being watched. When you are totally absorbed in a movie, there is only what's happening. You laugh and cry along with the movie as if it were happening to you. You forget yourself. You dissolve into the movie.

That's why we love going to movies. When you're watching a movie, you don't have to do a damn thing: you just let what's happening wash over you. Or more accurately, you are *washed away* by the movie. You and your past and future disappear in favour of what's happening. And because what's happening on the screen isn't essentially real, you can fully engage with the experience, you can fully let yourself go and enter into what's happening without reservation, and laugh and cry and cheer along with what's happening as if it were really happening. It's because it's not real that–for a while, anyway–it's fully real. This is the apparent paradox at the heart of

31

experience. Life is just one great big movie. The greatest movie ever made.

So in the waking up, the movie remains a movie. In the waking up, the dream remains a dream. It's not essentially real but when you're engrossed in it, it appears to be.

The story of 'you', your past and your future, isn't essentially real – it only appears to be when there is mesmerisation with the dream-movie of life. At any point in the story, the invitation is there to wake up from the story. In that, the story does not cease. It goes on, but is seen through. It becomes transparent. The movie continues to play, but it's seen for what it is.

And then you know that nothing that happens can ever hurt you. The sad scenes, the terrifying scenes, they cannot even make a scratch anymore.

You become very much like the screen on which the movie is projected: whatever happens in the movie, the screen is not tainted. It lovingly allows anything to be projected onto it. The scary scenes, the joyful scenes, all are allowed. And then the movie ends, and the audience leaves, and the screen is as fresh and clean as it was before the movie started.

And of course, from the perspective of the screen, nothing starts or ends at all! From the perspective of the screen, there is no time or space. The movie is the movie of time and space. When there is nothing being projected, time and space become meaningless.

In liberation, time and space are seen for what they are: concepts.

This book isn't about solving all of your problems. That's all in the dream. It's a dream character trying to solve dream problems. It's a character in a movie trying to solve his or her fictional movie problems.

The character in the movie believes that his or her problems are real. But of course, the problems are only as real as the character is. The actor finishes on set, removes his make-up, changes clothes and goes home. The DVD is ejected from the player, and everything vanishes. The reels of film are boxed up and put away, and the lights in the cinema are turned off. Your problems are only as real as you are.

Nobody There

Everything in your life is pointing to your own absence.

Even the most intense suffering is pointing to the absence of the one who suffers.

At the heart of the most intense suffering, right at the heart of it, there is simply nobody there who suffers. Even suffering is pointing to the absence of the separate, solid person. And that can be very difficult to hear. Bear with me.

There is pain, but there's nobody there who is in pain. That's the dream, that's the suffering: that there is a *person* here. No, there is only pain happening, only sensation happening, but nobody there to whom it's all happening. Only the present appearance of life, only present sights and sounds and smells, but nobody there at the centre of it all. Just an absence which is an absolute presence. Just nothing playing the game of being everything.

Thoughts are happening, but there is nobody there who is thinking.

There is a chair, but nobody sitting on it.

Right now, nobody is breathing. Nobody is seeing. Nobody is hearing. Breathing just happens. The room, the book, the words on the page just appear. The eyes open and they just appear. Sounds simply happen.

"I'm breathing, I'm seeing, I'm hearing"–that's the *story*.

Prior to the story, there is absolutely nothing. Before the story "I'm a person, sitting on a chair, reading a book" there is no person, no chair, no book. Prior to the 'I' story there is nothing, and nobody there to know that. Prior to the 'I', well, we cannot really say a damn thing about that. There is only the mystery. And even that isn't true.

And out of the mystery 'I' appears. And the moment you have an 'I', you appear to have something called a 'world'. Prior to that contraction, there is no world. The world arises with 'I'. Expansion, contraction. Creation, destruction. The heartbeat of the cosmos.

The Myth of Enlightenment

Liberation isn't something that I have and you don't. This message is not about awakened people or enlightened people passing on their understanding to others.

There are no awakened people, there are no enlightened people, because in reality there are no people at all.

People who believe that they are awakened, people who say "I'm awakened and you aren't" or "I see this and you don't", these people still believe in separation. "I'm awakened, you're not" – it's more separation than ever! In order to say that, there would still need to be a point of reference there, a 'me'. A 'me' comparing itself to a 'you'. A 'me' that wakes up every morning and reminds itself that it's awakened.

But when that whole 'me and you' game falls away, when those reference points are no longer there, all you are left with is the mystery.

When it all falls away, you have no way of knowing that you are awakened.

You have no way of knowing anything. You have no more words for what *this* is. Like a newborn baby, you see everything for the first time. And nothing has a name. Like Adam in the garden of Eden, you begin to name it all from scratch.

Awakened people, enlightened people, that's all in the

dream. It's the dream character who searches for awakening. And when that character finally finds awakening, it turns out to be a dream awakening.

Nothing Changes, Everything Changes

Even if you had this thing called awakening, what would you do with it? We can't even see the grace, the wonder of sitting in a chair. We can't even see what's directly in front of us with any clarity, so how the hell are we going to see this awakening, when we finally get it? We can't even see *this*! Even if we had something called awakening, we wouldn't be able to see that either.

Start with this. Start here. See *this* first.

And the funny thing is, when you see *this*, you don't even want *that* anymore.

Because when you see this, what you also see is that this is always enough.

Just sitting here on this chair, breathing, just this is enough. More than enough.

And in the seeing of this, an ordinary life can be led. There is still waking up in the morning, and putting on clothes, and walking out into the fresh air, and chopping wood, and carrying water, and doing all the things you used to do.

Nothing has changed: there is still a very ordinary life being led.

And yet, everything has changed, because the heaviness has gone, the seriousness has gone, the seeking has gone.

The seeker is dead.

Nothing has changed and everything has changed, and what is seen is that from the beginning there has only ever been the miracle.

This book is sharing a possibility: that the search of a lifetime can come to an absolute end with the falling-away of the sense of being a separate individual, and a plunge into Unconditional Love.

2
THE EXTRAORDINARY IN THE ORDINARY

There is no 'how' to be free.
If you ask 'how' to be free, you are not listening.

- J. Krishnamurti

Jeff, what is nonduality?

Well, that is *the* question, isn't it! To me, the word 'nonduality' means 'not two' and it points to the fact that somehow everything is One. Although it seems like there are separate things in the world, separate people, separate individuals; although it seems like there is a past and a future, and separate objects, actually it's all One. And the spiritual search is really the search *for* Oneness.

We realise that we want something more to feel complete. It's a very human thing in one way.

It is. And the seeking begins with a sense of separation. It's because I feel separate that I begin to seek. And in the material world, it's the search for money, fame, better relationships, a stronger sense of self. In the spiritual world, it's the search for awakening, enlightenment, liberation. But really it's all the same search.

It's the search for completion. The search for home. What I try to communicate is that you never left home in the first place. That Oneness is all there is. And it's here, and it's now, and we're not separate from it.

And in the seeing of that, the whole search for something more falls away.

And when that happens, what does it feel like?

43

(*Laughs*) You know, it's very difficult to talk about! When that happens – the falling away of the separate self – you are not there to experience it!

When you say "You are not there", what does that actually mean?

To put it simply, the past and the future aren't there. This heavy sense of myself as a separate person in the world isn't there. There's just what's happening.

And there's nobody there to know that. It just cannot be known. It's a plunge into the unknown, which is where we always are anyway.

But you still think? Thinking still happens?

Well, thoughts still arise. Thoughts are allowed to arise. But they aren't a problem anymore, because there's no longer anyone there using thoughts to build up an identity.

We grow up in the world, and we grasp at things. We try to make ourselves into something. That's really the human condition, you could say: the attempt to be someone, to be something, to possess, to grasp. When all of that falls away, everything is released, so that it can finally be itself, without the grasping. And in that, anything can arise, of course. Thoughts, sounds, smells, feelings in the body. But there's no sense that any of it is mine, no sense that I'm a separate entity in control of any of this.

So, sounds happen, but there's nobody there hearing. There's nobody there who thinks "I'm doing this! I'm hearing!" The 'me' at the centre of my life is seen to be an illusion. Life is seen to have no centre. But it doesn't mean that life ceases! People have this idea that when liberation happens, everything stops. No, absolutely not. This is an opening up. An opening up to what is. An allowing of what is. But it's not something that you are doing. And that's the hardest thing to hear!

What happens to your personality?

It's the personality that's seen through! What's seen is that there is nothing fixed there called 'me'.

But you still have your likes and dislikes, it's just that they are not dominating you?

Yes. It all becomes very playful. You play at being Jeff, when it's needed. This Jeff character, where is he? He's just a thought, happening now.

This isn't a special state that I'm in. It's true for all of us: you are just a thought. Your whole past and future is just a thought arising now.

Are you aware of the personality changing over time? Does it become more refined? Does it lose certain charges?

It's very difficult to talk about without making the Jeff character sound special. This is very ordinary. It's a collapse back into what there already was. It's always been here, we just couldn't see it. We were so lost in the seeking game that we couldn't see what was there in front of us.

I've spent some time with people who feel that they are in an enlightened space, awakened space, whatever you call it.

And there's no doubt that there's something special going on. And yet at times I would see that their personality would take over. I'm interested in the possibility of maybe the personality developing so it doesn't have any influence at all.

In the seeing of this, in the seeing that there is no 'me' at the centre of my life–and this is the foundation on which our whole lives are built–in this falling away, yes, the mind, or thought, or personality, whatever you want to call it, can still seem to have a momentum to it. All the mind has known is seeking. So that can come back in. It's like, the moment you think you're awakened, you're not. Because the mind is going to come back in.

Because you think you're awakened. You think you're special, you think you're separate.

Right. As long as you think you're awakened, or enlightened, or liberated, there's a 'you' there who thinks that. That idea of personal achievement is the hardest thing to let go of. For a long time, I thought that I was enlightened. And you know, that was just a belief. That was separation. "I'm enlightened, you're not!" Separation. And there was a sense of superiority there. I thought I had something special.

But all of that fell away too. It wasn't real. It was the final illusion to fall away. But it *was* an illusion. The ego loves to feel that it's enlightened. Then it can go round the world telling everyone it's enlightened!

Of course, it's a great party trick!

It is. And what was seen over here is that there is no 'I' who can be enlightened or not.

Does this stage – and I know that's not the right word – develop?
Does it evolve? Do you feel changes? Is there a movement?

There is only what's happening, and everything else
fades into the background. In *this*, it's already complete.
It's seen that life is already complete. And in that seeing,
the stuff that isn't real just falls away, it burns up. And
that can appear to take time. But what's seen in clarity is
that there is only now, there is only this. And so to talk
about the Jeff who changes, that just doesn't feel real to
me anymore.

I remember speaking to someone who'd had something very
significant happen to them. For them, it was like the back-
ground became the foreground and the foreground became the
background. Reference points shifted, things burnt away, and
life was seen from a different point of view.

But *this* has always been here. It's not a new reference
point. Babies see this. Newborn babies see this.

Because when they're born, they don't feel separate? They just
feel interconnectedness?

To a baby

They don't even feel that. There's just what's happening.
There's nobody there who says "I feel connected, I feel
at one with everything". No, there's just the spontaneity,
just what's happening. And as adults we seem to move
so far away from that spontaneity, that sense of aliveness, that simplicity. In our search to be someone, we
become very heavy, very serious. We miss this – what's
happening – because we're so busy looking for something
more, something for *me*.

Isn't that the game?

That's the game.

Is there any way out? Can babies stay in that space?

I expect it might be possible. But look, there are no mistakes in Oneness. The game has to play itself out. The separation, the suffering has to play itself out, in order to be seen. It's like the suffering and separation are there to wake us up. I look back at my life and the intense suffering and the intense seeking, and at the time it was horrible, but looking back, it just had to happen that way because it *did* happen that way, and not for any other reason. There are no mistakes.

Earlier we were talking about your life story. You went through difficult periods when you were very unhappy. And, understandably, you turned to meditation and self-enquiry in order to find a way out.

Absolutely. The search was the attempt to escape the misery I was experiencing. My whole life I'd been pretty miserable, but I reached a point of breakdown in my mid-twenties. There was such intense suffering and misery. The futility of everything was seen.

The futility of life, was that at the core of your misery?

Yes. It was the heaviness of being a separate person. I really felt that intensely. I was very lonely. I felt that the world didn't care about me. I could never find any relationships. I was very alone.

The game didn't work for you?

It didn't work.

I was blessed with a sharp intellect. I was quite clever I suppose. But apart from that, I hated myself, plain and simple. I hated the way I looked. Life felt like a burden. I didn't want to get out of bed in the morning. It was all too much. And I think I experienced that for most of my life. Of course I never fully realised at the time how miserable I was. At the time I just thought "This is who I am, this is my lot."

Did you do any work on your personality? People might argue that your personality wasn't properly formed, perhaps due to bad experiences in your childhood.

On the surface I had quite a *happy* childhood. My parents were lovely to me. I always had everything I needed. But on the inside it was all just too much for me. I hated who I was.

When you say you hated who you were, how did you see who you were?

Well that's the problem. I *knew* who I was!

So you felt separate from everybody else, and you felt there was something else out there you couldn't get in touch with?

I always felt like a very small person in a big world. I felt totally insignificant. And I think that's the separation taken to an extreme. That's where I ended up. We all feel that to an extent. We all feel like small people in a big world, a world of birth and suffering and old age and death.

We know we will die, but we think 'Not me!' For most of us death seems a long way off.

49

We try and push it aside. We try not to think about it. But it comes out in other ways you see. It comes out as suffering and anxiety.

The attempt to escape death is essentially the attempt to escape from being nothing. That's why we fear death: it's literally a plunge into nothingness. And nothingness cannot be known. And the mind operates in the realm of the known. We fear what we don't know.

What we don't understand?

Yes, it's the same. What we know, what we understand, we can control. And what death shows us is that there is no control. Death and illness have a funny way of showing us that there is something else going on here, something that's beyond our control. So that's why we spend our lives – and we don't recognise that we're doing it of course – trying to escape from the realisation that we are nothing. On some level we all know that we are nothing. We've all been newborn babies. We've all tasted that innocence, that lack of solidity, that openness, that sense of not being anything in particular.

And essentially that innocence, that freshness, that openness hasn't been lost. It's just become obscured by the seeking game, apparently. By the game of being a separate person, a person separate from the world. And it's out of that illusion, that assumption, that all suffering begins.

For me, the suffering and separation had reached a critical point, and that's when this other possibility started to shine through. In this particular case, it had to reach that point of absolute despair.

So it went to the extreme, and something was able to flip?

Yes, it was either transform or commit suicide. There was no other option.

That sounds pretty dramatic!

Yes. It was change or suicide.

Was that a decision you had to make?

In the telling of it, it always sounds like we have a choice. But of course, we never do. It had to happen the way it happened. There's no mistakes in this. That's the illusion, that's where all the suffering begins: with the sense that I'm a separate person who can choose. With the sense that things in the past could have happened differently. Which implies that *this* – what's happening now – shouldn't be the way it is. When it's seen that nothing could have happened differently, that's the same thing as saying that *this* has to be exactly the way it is. That *this* couldn't be otherwise.

When you reached that critical point, what happened next?

Well, I became quite sick, with a pretty serious case of glandular fever. And one night I collapsed in my bathroom. I had been vomiting blood, and I passed out. I woke up in a pool of blood, tried to move and realised that I was paralysed. And I thought, "That's it, I'm going to die."

And it was something about that – something about how precious this life is, and how quickly it can be wiped out – something about that stayed with me. A few days later, I was lying in hospital, feeling a lot better, and there was something about that experience that lingered. My whole life, I'd never realised how precious it was just to be alive. I'd taken it for granted. The simplicity of it, the fact that I'm alive at all, that had been ignored in my attempt to be *someone* in the world. Something about that experience in the bathroom had hit me, the taste of death and how close it was, and how easily all of this could fall away. Something about the impermanence of our lives. The illness had just come out of nowhere, out of nowhere. At the time, that terrified me: how easily all of this could be taken away.

For my whole life I'd been a committed atheist. The word 'spirituality' meant nothing to me. It meant witches and goblins and ghouls, I didn't know! Religion seemed ridiculous to me. And I remember there was a Bible by the side of my hospital bed, and I found myself just picking it up, and turning the pages, and reading the words of Jesus, and for the first time in my life they weren't just empty words, it wasn't just some man-made nonsense, there was something in it, something about Eternal Life, something about the preciousness of this, something about, well, something beyond. I didn't know at the time what it was, but there was a *resonance* there.

I didn't have a choice. That's where the spiritual seeking began. I had to find out what this was, this *resonance*. And I had to find it 'out there.'

And when you say the seeking began, what form did it take?

Well, I'd been a seeker my whole life. The individual *is* a seeker. But it was at that point that spiritual seeking began. I just found myself doing it. Once that fire had been lit, there was no way back. And I moved back to Manchester to stay with my parents whilst I recovered from my illness, and I shut myself off in my room for about a year.

That's quite extreme!

I was a very extreme person! (*Laughs*) I was blessed – or cursed, I don't know – with a very strong intellect. I'd been educated at Cambridge University. I was very clever, and so once I got my hands on something I had to tear it apart. I had to go right into it – that was my nature. Once that fire began, it was so intense, it just started to burn and I couldn't put it out.

I started with basic books on Buddhism, Christianity, basic books on meditation, self-enquiry, and then, oh, everything, I mean everything! I tried everything!

You mean you'd try a certain meditation technique for a time, a certain religion for a time...?

Yes, and I started to have all sorts of 'spiritual experiences'. Glimpses of Oneness, the dissolving of the self, intense compassion; sometimes I'd just break down in tears for hours on end at the sheer beauty of it all. And there were times of great despair too. Seeing the impermanence of everything. Seeing that I wasn't there. Seeing that the whole search might, in fact, be futile. It was a very dramatic time. Old beliefs started to fall away, beliefs that I'd had for a lifetime. I started to see that I wasn't who I'd thought I was.

Did you feel basically positive about what was happening?

I can't say I felt positive about it. At the start it was all very exciting, but it got pretty nasty towards the end. The seeking became so intense. But I knew I couldn't give it up. I knew that.

When you say intense, do you mean you would do more extreme things? You would meditate for longer and longer periods?

It was intense in the sense that I'd shut myself off from ordinary life. From ordinary human relationships. From the simple things. To be honest, I don't remember a lot about that time. So much happened, so much fell away. I became a militant vegan at one point! I was just exploring everything, looking for the answers. I knew the answers couldn't be found in the way I'd been living my life. And they couldn't be found in having a nice job, or finding a nice girl to marry. They couldn't be found in the ways or places I'd thought they could be found. It was a clear seeing of that.

It reached a point of such intensity that my whole identity was consumed by the fact that I was a spiritual seeker. That was *me*. I'd swapped my old identity for a new identity! I thought I was becoming free from all identity, but what I couldn't see then was that "I'm a spiritual seeker" was becoming more of an identity than ever. It was something else to cling to.

But it had opened your world. Given you new horizons.

The spiritual seeking had opened so much up. But there was still a sense of being a separate individual. In a way I think that sense was stronger than ever at that point. I wasn't as miserable anymore, but I suppose I was miserable in a different way. I was now miserable that I hadn't reached enlightenment. I was 'spiritually' miserable.

You were very driven!

Very. When people come to my meetings these days, and they ask me questions, well, I've already asked all those questions you see! I've done this seeking thing! I asked every question known to man and I never found the answers. Well, I did. I found plenty of answers... and then the seeking would start up again. There seemed to be this incessant movement into a future. This constant looking for something I thought I'd lost.

And it's seen so clearly now: as long as there was a separate person there looking for awakening, there was a separate person there! And that's what I couldn't seem to shake off: the separate person. No matter how hard I tried, I couldn't seem to get rid of this 'me', this separate 'me'. At one point, I'd seen it so clearly: as long as the 'I' was there, I couldn't awaken. So then the focus became getting rid of this 'I'. Getting rid of the self at the root of it all. What I couldn't see, then, was that it was a self trying to get rid of a self. Such vicious circles of thought!

And those circles became more and more subtle. The seeking went on in more and more subtle ways. As the seeking was seen through in one way, it changed form and carried on in a more subtle way. It's like the mind didn't want to give up. It didn't want to give up the idea that one day 'I' would eventually awaken.

And all I can say is that somehow, in the midst of all that, the whole thing fell away. But I certainly can't say that it was because of something I did. In my effort to create that falling away, I'd just been reinforcing the sense of 'me'.

But if you hadn't made that effort, would it all have fallen away?

Well, that is the central question, isn't it? What was seen so clearly was that it was already here, already complete. The awakening, Oneness, whatever you want to call it, was already here. But it wasn't something that I could *have*. It couldn't be possessed, it couldn't be grasped. And it was in the grasping, in the attempt to possess it, that I'd apparently lost it.

It's a terrible dilemma for a spiritual seeker. On the one hand, you can't get it. On the other hand, you can't stop trying. You still have to live your life, follow your heart, go where your life is taking you; you still have to do that, and that's the amazing adventure. And it's very inspiring to meet someone like you, who did all this, and then something opened, something changed. And your unhappiness, your depression, dropped away, for whatever reason.

But you see, the beauty of this, is that it was seen right *in the midst* of that despair.

Yes, I get that.

I thought I had to overcome despair *before* I could awaken. What was seen is that this was *already here*, right at the heart of what I'd taken to be my life, right at the heart of the despair. It was seen that it wasn't 'my life' at all. That no matter what was happening, there was a freedom there that could never leave, because it wasn't something that I *had*. It was something that was just there, and it had nothing to do with 'me'.

It's like it just sits there, and allows the seeking to play itself out. Throughout all my seeking and suffering, there had only ever been Oneness, and yet I hadn't been able to see it. And yet even though I hadn't seen it, there had still only ever been Oneness!

And yet this whole seeking and suffering game had played itself out perfectly. That was seen too: that it couldn't have been otherwise. The seeking had exhausted itself when it was ready. When *it* was ready. And it had nothing to do with me.

I remember when I first saw it in a chair. I was in my bedroom at home, looking at a chair, and I realised that I'd never seen a chair before. I'd been too busy looking for something more! Something for 'me'. Something so much more than the chair. I'd been looking for enlightenment, liberation, awakening. Always in the future. And so I'd missed the chair.

And something funny happened. It was like the chair revealed its secrets. In the falling away of the seeking, the chair revealed its secrets. It was Oneness disguised as a chair! It wasn't a chair at all! We call it a chair so we don't have to see it. "Oh, I *know* it's a chair, I *know* it's a table..." But when all of that falls away, it's like nothing can be known about it. It's not a chair. It is what it is. Everything becomes very alive. And yet we can still call it a chair. We can still use ordinary language. We can still function as if we were leading a very ordinary life. And yet, underneath, it's all the miracle. It's nothing like you thought it would be. The moment you have an idea of what this is, it's just an idea. This is too alive to ever be captured, to ever be known.

And you had a few of these... experiences. You mentioned in your book Beyond Awakening *that you were walking through the rain in Oxford one day, and realised that you were everything and that you were home. Did these situations arise more frequently and get stronger?*

When this was first seen, it was all very dramatic. It was shocking, to see that the secret had been here from the beginning, right at the heart of a very ordinary life. That the extraordinary had always been hidden in the ordinary, in the most ordinary of things. And when that was first seen there was a great excitement, there was a drama about it.

These days, it's all become very ordinary. It's become very gentle. It's always there in the background. It's not so dramatic. It's like the whole thing collapsed back down into a very ordinary life, on the surface anyway. At the time, there were all sorts of experiences. Walking in the rain that day in Oxford, there was just love. That was all there was. Everything was a manifestation of that, and nothing was separate from what I took to be myself. And at the time that was very new and very dramatic. But all that's died away now, it's very gentle now.

Was there any fear when these things happened?

When the person falls away, there's just what is, and it's all so clear, so obvious. And it cannot be known, and it cannot be spoken of, but it's undeniably the case.

And then the mind can come back in. It's only then that

it begins to write and talk about it. It says "I had an experience. That happened to *me*." Actually *you* weren't there at all! It didn't happen to *you*! It's out of fear that the mind comes back in and tries to grasp. It tries to create structure there, so it can feel secure.

The reason I ask, is that I read this book a few years ago, 'Collision with the Infinite' by Suzanne Segal, and she had, it would appear, a similar experience. But she also had tremendous anxiety. Presumably the anxiety is something to do with the mind?

Yes, it's still the mind trying to hang on. It's perhaps the last tactic the mind uses. It uses the fear tactic. "There's something to fear! There's something to fear!" Actually, there's just the fear. Just fear arising. There's nothing *to* fear.

Where you are these days, do you have fear and anxiety sometimes?

Anything can arise here. Fear and anxiety, no, not really anymore. But the point is that *everything* is allowed in this. Anger, fear, joy, sadness everything is allowed. It can all come. It's as if anything is allowed to arise exactly when it arises, because there's just nobody there trying to resist it, fight it, get an identity out of it. Say, if your mother died, there might be sadness there. People have this idea that liberation is a state in which you don't really feel anything. That it's a place of nothingness, where nothing can affect you. That's a load of bull! That's another idea, another concept. Oneness allows everything. How could it not? It *is* everything! So sadness can be there. And when sadness is there, there is sadness! But there is nobody there trying to do anything with sadness. And then a funny thing happens: the sadness lives its own little life, and burns itself up, in its own time.

There's no charge to it?

There's no charge. And in that, sadness can be fully sad! In the midst of sadness, it can be seen that there is sadness there and yet there is no sadness there. This is a place the mind could never go. There's sadness there, but because there is nobody there who is sad – there is no sad person – actually the sadness isn't there at all. Even to call it sadness, there already has to be a person there calling it something, labelling it.

It's impossible to talk about, and impossible to understand. That there is sadness there, and no sadness there, at the same time.

It's a lack of identification, isn't it? Is it like you're just watching it?

Everything is being registered. It's effortless. We think we are doing the hearing, doing the seeing, doing the breathing. Actually this is all just happening, effortlessly. There's an intelligence here that's totally beyond the mind. The mind hasn't a hope of grasping this. It's what's beating the heart. It's what's breathing.

The human body is an incredible, intricate mechanism.

And the hardest thing to hear is that the body doesn't need us. It doesn't need our seeking, it doesn't need our suffering, it doesn't need our identity. It functions effortlessly without us. It's the hardest thing to hear, for someone who's so attached to their teachings, to their games of becoming, to hear that you are irrelevant, that you are absent.

And yet, it's not a cold, dead, detached absence. It's a very alive, very full absence. It's an absence that's full of everything that's happening. Actually, that absence is a perfect presence. So we talk about being present, being in the now. But when you're fully present, 'you' are not there. So really 'you' cannot be present. It's not something that 'you' can do. Presence is there in the absence of 'you'.

That's one of the first things you learn when you go on the spiritual path: to be present.

Yes, but what was seen here is that there is *only* presence. It's not something that you can have, or get closer to. And everything is already happening within that presence. Even the seeking and the not-being-present is happening in the most perfect presence! Presence is already embracing everything. It denies nothing, it resists nothing. It allows even the most intense suffering to play itself out.

In the image of Jesus on the cross, we see that at the heart of the most intense suffering known to man, right at the heart of that is eternity. Eternity is not to be found through an escape from suffering—it's right at the heart of suffering. So right at the heart of the most intense suffering it can be seen that there's nobody there who suffers.

But there appears to be a lot of suffering in the world. Recently on the television we've seen a lot of suffering in Burma and China with the cyclone and the earthquake. People have lost

61

their homes and loved ones, people are injured and there's no medical help. Does that affect you at all?

It's myself in Burma, it's myself in the earthquake. It's myself starving in Africa. People sometimes hear the message of nonduality and they think that it's about sitting back and doing nothing. They think it's about arrogantly sitting back and saying "Oh, it's just a dream, it's just a story, there's nobody there suffering so what's the point in doing anything at all?"

Actually in the clear seeing that there's nobody here who suffers, and that suffering is just a story, there can be *effortless action* to help where help is needed. But it comes from a place where you just don't know. It comes out of the not knowing. Oneness recognises itself in the face of that starving child and can move to help itself, not out of pity, not because it needs to be a good person; that's nothing to do with it. It doesn't come from a set morality. But in the seeing that it's all One – and this is the mystery of the universe – somehow it moves to help itself. Because it only sees itself, as the starving child, as the earthquake victim. And so it moves to do something, if that's possible.

Or not. It might not move, you see. There's just no way of knowing. It comes from a place of no thought. It doesn't come from a place where I'm separate from you and I'm suffering because you're suffering, and I feel pity for you, and I want to be a good person. No, the universe doesn't need that. It doesn't need our pity. It doesn't need our suffering on top of their suffering.

So, to see it all in clarity is to end it. And then there may be a movement to help, or not.

And what form might that movement take?

There's no way of knowing in advance. The moment you have an idea of what you should do to help, the moment you have a set agenda, you stop seeing. For example, if you think that the most important thing in the world is to save the Amazon rainforests, and that's all you ever think about, you might miss that little old lady who is crossing the road right now and needs your help in this moment. Because you're coming from a set idea of what's right and what's wrong, you might miss that old lady who's more important than all the rainforests put together, because she's right here in front of you, and she is yourself too.

So there's no structure to it, and I don't understand it, nobody understands it, it's just the mystery of creation. Somehow it recognises itself. It's God seeing himself everywhere.

So what motivates you? You do talks, and you write books. What keeps you going?

I really don't know where it comes from. If I'm honest, the way it feels is that it's all just happening. It's all beyond my control. Jeff could never have done this. The moment Jeff had tried to make this happen, he would have failed miserably. And it might sound like I'm trying to be clever by saying that, but that's really what it feels like. It really feels effortless. It's just unfolding, evolving, and I really don't know how it's happening or why it's happening but it's happening. This expression of non-duality seems to come out of this mouth, and it's always a surprise.

You were saying earlier that you used to be very shy. You studied Astrophysics at Cambridge University and you did that partly because you didn't want to have to communicate with people! And here you are talking away no problem!

(*Laughs*) I know! It's astonishing. I just don't know. I sit in my meetings, and talking to you now, and the words just come out. If I could put it into words, it's like I sit back and just watch these words come out. And sometimes they surprise me. Sometimes I'm shocked at what comes out. There's the sense that "I couldn't have done this, I wouldn't have said this."

When you listen to the real geniuses of our time, the Einsteins of this world, they say that they don't really create their own ideas, that their ideas just come out of nowhere.

It all emerges out of nothing.

You're like a vehicle.

But it's nothing to do with 'me'. It all seems to emerge effortlessly. It's talking about itself! There's no effort in talking about this because there's nothing to talk about! What we're talking about here is nothing. It's no object. It can't be pinned down. The moment we utter the first word about this, we're already into the dream. And once that's seen in clarity, once it's seen that this cannot be spoken of, the words just emerge freely again, and don't ask me how! They seem to come. And if I could put it into words, I sit back and watch the words come out, and I don't know what's going to come out next.

A lot of artists talk about this: when they're in the flow, when they're really into what they're doing, the art just comes out of nowhere, it does itself, it emerges from nothing. It's like we're at the point of creation and destruction, and it's all happening now. This is creation and destruction, and it cannot be *known*.

And that's the beauty of it: if it could be *understood*, it would be a thing. It would be a concept. This is just pure not-knowing. And in the absence of seeking the mystery reveals itself, and not just in the talking but in everything. In these flowers, and this floor, and this chair, and this table. It's everything. Everything is the mystery.

It's something coming out of nothing. The very fact that this is happening at all, this is the miracle.

From a mathematical point of view, if our planet was just a tiny bit different from the way it is, it couldn't host human life. And that's one of the things we forget: the delicate balance of everything. That's the feeling I get from you: everything just happens, and we don't know why it happens but it is the way it is. And some kind of shift in you happened all those years ago, and not much happened but it was so significant. It's about realising how intricate and delicate and fine everything is.

And how precious it is.

Yes.

And how far away we move from that in our seeking, in our search to be *someone*. The preciousness right at the heart of life. The preciousness that's always there. We miss it. We're too busy looking for something.

Really nothing happened to me. Nothing changed. There's still an ordinary life being lived. There's just nobody living that life. It's being lived. It's living itself. It's Oneness playing itself out in the form of an apparent separate person. Essentially there's no difference between you and me. It's Oneness 'looking out' through these eyes and Oneness 'looking out' through those eyes. And Oneness has no preferences. It's equally 'happy' looking through *these* eyes or hearing through *these* ears as it is looking through *those* eyes or hearing through *those* ears.

The only thing that separates us, apparently, is the story of 'me'. A story which is so fragile it can fall away just like that, leaving only presence. It's the miracle that's right at the heart of things, right there in the midst of the messiness of human life. And when that's seen it's shocking because it destroys all seeking, leaving you here, totally present and totally absent.

And people get so lost. That's so sad in one way, and amazing in another way.

But it really couldn't be any other way. Maybe the suffering and seeking are there to show us this. Maybe nothing is out of place, and right from the Big Bang and the preciousness and fragility of that, nothing has been out of place.

Interview by Iain McNay
Conscious TV
www.conscious.tv

this...

I am talking to a woman. She is telling
me about a passion of hers. Her dream
is that one day she will own and run a
small hotel, a bed and breakfast by the
sea. I notice that her eyes begin to well
up with tears as she relates her dream
to me. And then I notice that these eyes
start to well up with tears too. It's like
what's happening *there* is being mirrored
here. Because there is nothing to get in
the way, what is left here is just a total
openness to others, just an open space
which welcomes everything that appears.
Her eyes well up, my eyes well up, what's
the difference?

When there is nobody here, there is
nothing to block 'you' out. Because there
is no 'me', there is no separate 'you'
either. There are just voices, faces, the
welling up of tears, or not. Just what's
happening. What's happening fills all
space. As that woman relates her story to
me, I become her. I long to own a little
bed and breakfast by the sea. It is my
heart's true desire. I feel the passion
deep within my bones, and the tears come.

I'm watching television. It's a game show.
A man has just won a large sum of money.

He says he is going to use it to take his family on holiday. They've never been on holiday before. The man laughs and shouts and weeps with joy. This laughs and shouts and weeps with joy. There is nothing to separate us. Oh, my family will be so happy when they find out!

Images of famine on the television. A young Somali girl, all skin and bone, with hollowed out eyes and sticks for arms, gazes into the camera. There is nothing to block that poor child out. I am the child. I am gazing at myself. She enters me, and everything heals itself.

I am on the train. A large bald-headed man starts to shout at me for no reason. I think he is drunk. He shakes his fists. His face is red with anger. I am the man. I feel the anger, the violence, and underneath it, the anxiety, the fear, the contraction that goes along with being a separate person. I have been this man. I am this man now. He is myself, coming to meet me on the 12.23 to Brighton.

And then the woman stops talking about her bed and breakfast dreams, and the tears are wiped out. There is no memory of them. Everything is wiped clean, and it begins again.

The game show ends, and I change channels on the television, and it's now a shopping

channel, and the laughter and joy and
money and family are wiped out, and
now there is only fascination with item
number 176387, *what beautiful colours*! It
becomes absorbed in the shopping channel,
and the game show vanishes without a
trace. The game show might have happened
a million years ago for all I care: *this*
replaces everything.

The doorbell rings and I walk away from
the image of the starving child. It's my
friend at the door. The starving child is
wiped out, and my friend replaces her. The
beauty of this is that it's everything and
it's nothing. It's no particular thing.
One thing replaces another, and there's no
way of knowing what's coming next. Friend
replaces dying child, brother replaces
friend, shopkeeper replaces brother,
cat replaces shopkeeper. It emerges out
of the Unknown, innocently, playfully,
ceaselessly.

I walk away from the angry man. The anger
disappears immediately. It's like it
never happened. Something else takes its
place. And then something else. And then
something else. There's enough space here
for an entire world. Joy, anger, fear,
sadness, laughter, tears. Everything is
welcome here.

I have no way of blocking life out
anymore. Because there is nobody here,

there is only raw, unedited, uncensored, unfiltered experience. And you can't even call it an 'experience': there's nobody here to experience anything. There's just *this*, happening to no-one. Nobody sheds tears, nobody senses anger, nobody watches television.

But it's not an empty void. It's a space that's constantly filled by life. By the woman who wants the bed and breakfast by the sea, by the starving child, by my friend at the door. You provide the solidity that I lack. The story of time and space is dead here, but you keep it going for me. There's nobody here, but then you enter the picture, and suddenly 'There is nobody here' is-like any concept-not true.

When you are not, what else is there but to be all that is?

When the witness collapses into everything that's witnessed, when awareness collapses into its contents, all that remains is a deep and total fascination with whatever is happening.

3
CONFESSIONS I

There is only *this*. Only what's happening.

To the person, that can sound terribly depressing.
And yet, when heard in clarity,
it's explosively liberating.

* * *

In liberation, life goes on,
it's just that you're not there anymore.

Life lives itself,
as it always has done.

* * *

* * *

It's the shift from
a person sitting on a chair,
to sitting on a chair just happening.

The shift from a person walking down the street,
to walking down the street just happening.

From a person living their life, to life just happening.

This shift doesn't happen in time.

In truth, it's already happening.

* * *

The one reading these words is the one who wrote them.

The answer to everything is contained in that sentence.

* * *

How wonderful it is to have no idea
what is going to happen.

To let life surprise you.

To wake up every morning like a newborn baby,
with the past wiped clean.

To know that everything will happen
exactly as it should.

To know that there is nothing higher,
more spiritual or more noble
than getting out of bed in the morning,
brushing your teeth,
putting on clothes and walking out into the fresh air.

To understand that there is nothing to understand.

To live every day, every hour, every moment
and know that it is always
your *last* day, *last* hour, *last* moment.

And to know that the last day is also the *first* day,
and the last moment the *first* moment.

To see presence in each and every little thing.

To look at the world and see only
a love with no name reflecting back at you.

* * *

* * *

People sometimes ask me "Jeff, what's it like for you? What's it like being awakened? What's it like being in a place of Oneness?" I find these questions impossible to answer. I simply don't know what it's like. All those questions are directed at a person, and there isn't one here. Enlightened? Awakened? Oneness? That's all for the person. When there's nobody here, there's nobody here to get enlightened, there's nobody who could awaken, there's nobody who could know anything about something called Oneness.

On the other hand, it would be silly to deny that something has changed here. Years ago, there was a separate, solid, miserable little self, who hated himself and feared the world, who couldn't stop thinking, who couldn't sleep at night because his mind was so active. These days, all of that is gone. But you see, nothing has come to take its place. It's not that Jeff was miserable and now he is happy. That's a wonderful story, but it has nothing to do with liberation. True, these days life is light, playful, a dance, not serious at all (and those words don't begin to capture it). But to say 'Jeff is happy' would be to fall horribly back into duality. 'Jeff is happy' and 'Jeff is miserable' arise and dissolve together. When one goes, the other goes too. And when both are gone, you have no way of knowing who or what you are.

And that is total freedom. Freedom to be anything. Freedom to be this. Freedom to be that. Freedom to be happy. Freedom to be sad. Freedom to be exactly what you are. But it's not a practice. It's not about *trying* to be what you are, *trying* to be at one with what's happening. No, what falls away is the trying, the effort, the contraction.

Jeff was depressed and now he isn't? No, what fell away was the sense of being Jeff at all, depressed or not! What fell away was the sense of being a separate person at all. And yet – and here's the part where it all seems very paradoxical – the Jeff character is not lost. *The character continues to function.* Liberation is not the loss of character, the loss of personality. It's not about depersonalisation or sitting back and being detached from life (and that is such a common trap in the spiritual search). No, part of this freedom is that the character is released too. The character is released and finally allowed to be itself, no holds barred.

And so when questions are asked, there is a response here. That's the character functioning. When someone asks "Jeff, what's your preference, red or white wine?", the response that often comes is "White, please." Preferences continue to function. Out of nothing, it speaks: "White, please." And when someone calls out in the street "Hey, Jeff!", the head turns and the mouth smiles and something here says "Hi!" back, and that's part of the mystery too. Nobody here, somebody here. This cannot be contained by either of those conceptual positions.

I would never go round saying "There is no self here" or "I have no ego", because of course, in order to say that, there would have to be a self here, an ego here that knows something about itself. When the reference point of the 'I' drops away, you cannot say anything about yourself. And yet, words may come out. But they are no longer your words. It's as though the functioning on the level of words and language goes on, but there can no longer be any mesmerisation with it. Words are used, but they can never be believed. And so, you ask my name, and I say "Jeff", or something says "Jeff" and it's as simple as that.

Right there, right there in normal, everyday interactions, the miracle shines. We don't need to fly off to India or meditate for the next thirty years in order to see it. It's already happening.

* * *

I never gave up spiritual practices. They fell away of their own accord, in their own time, when it was seen that the one who sits down to meditate is identical with the one who sits down to have a pint of beer at the local pub. Already, nobody sits down to meditate, and already nobody has a beer. I used to believe that meditating was somehow 'higher' or more 'spiritual' than drinking beer. But those divisive concepts went out the window when the shocking equality of every action was seen. And in that, meditation just fell away, and self-enquiry became obsolete. These days, I have no interest in meditation, in being present or getting in touch with the silence or anything else. Life—as it is—is always enough.

Of course, if you do want a spiritual practice, I'll give you one...

Oh look, you're already doing it.

* * *

* * *

Living like this, how do you function in the world? How do you live?

It's not a question you ever need to ask. Somehow, it all takes care of itself. Somehow, things get done. It wakes up in the morning, it puts on clothes, it eats when it's hungry. I have no way of separating myself from what's happening. What's happening is myself, which is another way of saying that there is no person here.

And yet, the character Jeff Foster continues to function, to live his life, and it's such a gift. All the questions just fall away. Never do I ask myself how to relate to life, because that question no longer makes any sense to me. There is only life playing itself out, only the vastness, only nothing playing the game of being everything.

And of course, those words don't even touch it. It's the intimacy that will never be put into words. Intimacy with breathing, with the heart beating, with the body, with the chair, with the table, with the trees and flowers, with everything, as it is. And it's all mine, and none of it is mine, and that apparent paradox dissolves into the absolute simplicity of what is.

Jesus said you have to lose your life to save it, and when everything is lost, when there are no longer any questions, when all the seeking falls away, you are simply left with the mystery of it all, and everything is wiped clean, and with the eyes of a child you look at the world, always for the first time, and see only love in its infinite guises.

* * *

If there is truly nobody there, isn't it a lie to say "Jeff" when somebody asks you your name?

When you go to the theatre to see an actor in a play, you don't accuse the actor of lying. He is honestly and truthfully *playing* at being the king, *playing* at being the pauper, *playing* at being the spiritual seeker. He is *playing* at being Jeff. In the play, when the character is asked "Who are you?", the character replies "Jeff". It is absolute honesty. This is nothing playing at being everything. This is nobody playing at being somebody. And in liberation, somebody and nobody are not two. Those dualistic concepts simply dissolve into the wonder of what's happening, into the wonder of the play.

And so when you ask "What's your name?", and this replies "Jeff", there is no contradiction whatsoever. This is no longer at war with the world.

And the play goes on.

* * *

I am Jeff. I am not Jeff. Equal.

There's nobody here, and yet when you look over here and ask "What is your name?", something here replies "Jeff".

Who replies? There is only that question. No response arises to meet it, and so the question dissolves back into the Source.

"What is your name?" the Source asks itself. Nothing really happens at all.

When you ask me what I did yesterday, the story of yesterday is told. Of course, there is no yesterday. Yesterday is a story happening now. Tomorrow is a story happening now. And yet, when you ask that question, the response is not "Yesterday is a story–your question makes no sense!" but "I went swimming. What did you do?" The answer arises to meet the question. Story meets story, effortlessly. This intimacy rejects nothing.

It's very simple. I just don't want anything. Whatever happens is okay.

This happens, *okay*. That happens, *okay*. It just doesn't really matter anymore. And that's freedom. It's like when you're watching a movie. Does it really matter what happens to the central character? If you're engrossed in the movie, yes. But when you realise that the movie is just a movie, no, it doesn't really matter, because the character doesn't really die, he doesn't really fall off a cliff, he doesn't really *do* anything at all.

It's the paradox of nothing appearing as everything. Nothing happens and everything happens. Nothing matters and everything matters. And really, there is no paradox at all, there is only the simplicity of life happening right now. Breathing, heart beating, sounds in the room, sensations in the body – that's it, full stop.

* * *

* * *

The whole thing comes to an end when you see that sitting on the toilet, or making a cup of tea, or taking a walk in the rain, is the most spiritual thing of all.

* * *

And ultimately, yes, before you ask, even 'Oneness' is just another concept.

* * *

I look across the table at my wife, Amy. And yet, of course, she's not 'mine' at all. There is nothing here that could possibly possess *anything*, let alone another person. There's nobody over there to possess anyway. She is my story, and I am hers. She is a character in my dream, and I'm a character in hers. I look across the table and what I see is a girl drinking a cup of tea. 'My wife' is just a story. What is actually there? A girl drinking a cup of tea, right now. Yes, right now, this is all there is. Where is this thing called 'our relationship'? All I can find is what is happening presently. A boy and a girl drinking tea together.

And not even that. Even 'boy and girl drinking tea together' is a story. There is only this: breathing, heart beating, sounds, colours, tea cups chinking, warm tea, voices, light, heat. This is all there is. And in this, there is never anything to separate us. So often in life something called 'relationship' comes between us, clouding the intimacy that has nothing to do with two separate people. It's like a third entity hovering there between the two of us. Me, you, and 'our relationship'. Our needs, our wants, our expectations of each other.

What happens when all of that falls away? What happens when all that carry-over from the past is rendered irrelevant? Then there is just this–a girl sitting there, drinking a cup of tea and talking, and her talking is aimed somewhere over here. It's so incredibly simple. It's the most uncomplicated thing in the world. Because she isn't mine, there is no 'relationship' to defend here. Nothing to worry about, nothing to hold onto. No sense of possession at all.

Because she isn't mine, I can see her in absolute clarity for what she really is. Because there's nothing there getting in the way, there is the space to really listen, to really see, to just be here, drinking this tea, enjoying this moment together, which is all there is anyway.

Because she isn't my wife, there is only unconditional love. How unbelievably precious. How unbelievably simple.

And what freedom in that! There is simply nothing here keeping us together. We both have the absolute freedom to walk away. And yet, we haven't yet. I'm always amazed by that: she has the absolute freedom to walk away, but she hasn't yet. Maybe one day she will. Maybe one day I will. Maybe it will be tomorrow. Who knows what the future may bring? But for now, there is a girl sitting over there, sipping her tea, and what is left is a simple gratitude for her being here. I know she doesn't have to be (because she is free) but she is. I know I don't have to be (because I am free) but I am.

It's all so very innocent: she's just a girl, sitting there drinking tea, telling me about her day. There's no desire to possess any of it. It is what it is, and it's enough. Who needs a 'relationship' when this grace is already here?

And yet, if you ask, I'll tell you that she's 'my wife'. It's my shorthand way of saying all of the above!

* * *

The eyes open, and I am looking out the window of an airplane. London Gatwick Airport is there, and I am that. The eyes blink, and Amsterdam obliterates London. I become Amsterdam, and this plane hasn't gone anywhere. The scenery has changed, that's all.

Without the names, nothing is even happening. Without the names, there is only the rumble of the plane's engine, a funny feeling in the stomach as the plane dips, Amy's head on my shoulder, her soft breathing and the vague smell of vomit from the couple in front as we descend into Gatwick, Schipol, Charles de Gaulle.

Raw, unfiltered experience is timeless. London appears and disappears without a trace; Amsterdam arises and falls away. California melts into Manchester, which arrives for a short stay and then packs its bags and leaves.

"Ladies and gentlemen, we are beginning our descent into nowhere. Please ensure your tray tables are in the upright position." I look out of my window again. In total stillness, clouds slice through the plane's wing.

We never travel and we never arrive. Even an eight-hour plane journey cannot get you one inch away from home.

Who am I?

What is the 'I'?

You'll search for the rest of your life, and all you'll end up finding is a first person singular pronoun.

You'll find a sound: *aiiiiieeee*.

You'll find a thought: 'I'.

But nothing behind it.

And that's liberation.

* * *

The life you are trying to understand is identical with the 'you' that is trying to understand it.

* * *

Liberation: a relaxation into *this*.

* * *

We think that freedom consists in having what we want.

But the moment you have something, there is insecurity: you may lose what you have.

True freedom is the loss of everything.

Because when you have nothing, there is nothing to lose.

This is the end of fear.

And when nothing is yours, everything is yours.

This is the end of war.

And when you are nothing, you are also everything.

This is the end of all seeking.

* * *

The moment I think or say something, I know that the opposite of what I think or say could also be true. Then the opposites are no longer at war. Then they complement each other rather than threaten each other. Then you get to *play* with the opposites.

Then life becomes playful, and words are no longer the enemy.

* * *

What should you do with your life? It's always the wrong question. Wait and see what *life* does.

"But this will lead to inaction and passivity!" you say. Well, what I find is that action happens. It breathes. It moves. It gets out of bed. It brushes its teeth. It plans, or doesn't. It talks, or doesn't. It travels, or doesn't. The Mystery has its own way. Fall madly in love with it all. Or don't. The Mystery remains a Mystery either way.

It is the *seeker* who is passive.

* * *

I used to think that it was very important to have something called a *purpose*. I spent years trying to find this purpose. I made myself very miserable in doing so. Everyone else seemed to have one, but I couldn't find mine.

How wonderful to see that life needs no purpose. That its purpose is its purposeless present appearance. Does music have a purpose? Does a sunset have a purpose? Does dancing have a purpose? Its purpose is in the listening, in the seeing, in the dancing. Life is at once meaningful and meaningless. It's both and it's neither.

How wonderful to see that my purpose – if there is any such thing – is just to be sitting here, breathing, heart beating, sounds happening. What awesome freedom in that.

* * *

* * *

Wanting is equivalent to lacking. *This* is already complete in itself; it is already the abundance you seek. When there is a mesmerisation with wanting, a sense of lack is experienced. And then we think that in order to put an end to the sense of lack, we need to get what we want. But getting what we want doesn't end the sense of lack for long.

We don't really want what we want. What we really want is an end to our sense of lack. But we try to use the wanting mechanism to get there.

In the complete falling away of the wanting, the sense of lack goes too. And it's seen in clarity that *this* lacks nothing. It's already totally full. It's already being itself perfectly.

As the Zen master asked: "In this moment, what is lacking?"

* * *

* * *

Love is when there is nothing between us. And there is never anything between us. There is *only* love.

* * *

Liberation is not an event that happens in time. Liberation is the falling away of the person who is waiting for that event!

Liberation is the falling away of the search for liberation.

Liberation is the end of liberation. What a wonderful paradox.

Liberation is not just another experience. Experiences come and go. It's the falling away of the one who experiences. The falling away of the experiencer. That could never be something that you experienced, even if you lived for another billion years.

* * *

I look at a flower. Except there is no 'I' doing the looking, and no flower to be seen. And yet, and yet, look – who could deny that undeniably flowery loveliness? Who could deny anything? Flower or no flower, there is *this*, right here, right now, beyond thought, beyond the intellect, beyond words. To say that there is no flower is to deny the flowery loveliness. To say that there is a flower is to shatter reality in one fell swoop, to put boundaries and borders and separation where there are none.

A flower or not? That question is already too much. The answer is already shining, and it has nothing to do with words.

A flower or not? Be careful! If you answer, or if you don't, the Zen master will cut your head off!

A flower or not? *Chop!*

* * *

* * *

I remember when I saw my dad for the first time. I saw him not as my father, not as 'mine' in any way, but simply as a character in a movie, a part being played by Being itself. I saw him in clarity, I saw what was actually there. I saw through the story, the story of father and son, the story that he wasn't who I wanted him to be, the story of *shoulds* and *shouldn'ts* and *might haves*. When all that heaviness dropped away, when the past became as irrelevant as the future, what was left was shockingly innocent: an old man, greying hair, wrinkles all over his face, liver spots on his hands. At once all attempts to change him ceased, and there was only gratitude for what was there.

It was all so innocent. He had been so innocent. I had been so innocent. He wasn't my father at all, and I wasn't his son. Those were just roles that we had mistaken for reality. The actor in the play had forgotten that he was an actor. He had forgotten that he had just been playing the role of father or son. He had become identified with the role, and reality had become totally constricted.

But now, the fog had cleared, the doors of perception had been cleansed, and all there was, was the simplicity of what was happening. Old man, greying hair, sitting on chair, eating breakfast. No sense that he was mine. No sense of possession. No sense of control or lack of it. Just an innocent character, being himself perfectly. Jesus said that he and the father were one, and now I knew what he'd meant.

In a sense, it was a death. Death of the father story, and

along with it, death of the son story. Death of father and son. Death of everything that had come between us. Death of the roles. Death of the pretence. Death of the façade, the masks, the games. And in that death, there was only the throb of life. Nothing real can ever die.

And not just father, but mother, sister, brother, friend, lover: all are just temporary roles. And those roles can be very useful when it comes to functioning in this world, but they can so easily come between us. They can so easily mask the intimacy that is always there.

When nothing is yours, everything is yours. When nothing is yours, there is nothing there that can block anything out. When nothing is yours, the world comes crashing in, in its purest form. Because there is no longer anything there blocking out the world, there is absolute *intimacy* with that world, with apparent others, with anything that arises.

Because the roles of father and son were no longer there, nothing could block out that intimacy any longer.

Oh, the intimacy with that little man eating his cornflakes! It's too exquisitely beautiful to even begin to talk about.

* * *

* * *

There is nothing to fear, because there is nobody here.

* * *

In liberation, heart and mind are not experienced as being separate.

So often nonduality can seem so heady, so conceptual, so intellectual. All those concepts of nothingness and absence and presence! Actually this is all about *love*. Love is the union of heart and mind.

Nonduality isn't about being detached from the world, being the witness of everything and taking part in nothing. It's not about sitting on your mountaintop and looking down at the world, pitying those poor mortals who aren't as awakened as you are, those poor souls who still have egos! No, love cannot stand back from the world, because it *is* the world.

The heart of presence radiates love.

* * *

* * *

Out of nothing, all of this appears. Where it comes from, and where it's heading, nobody knows.

Nobody knows a thing about it, and yet it's all given for free. This is an act of pure love.

You don't need to understand any of these words. Just dissolve into the mystery of it. Melt into what the words are pointing to.

Sacrifice your understanding. It has already served its purpose.

* * *

* * *

This is beyond existence and non-existence. It's beyond self and no-self. It's beyond subject and object, time and space, past and future. All those words become redundant when the taste of your cup of tea, or the *tweet-tweet* of a bird, or the roar of the traffic becomes the most fascinating thing in the world.

* * *

Subject and object arise together and dissolve together.

And yet, in truth, there is no subject, and no object.

There is only what's happening. And even that is saying too much.

* * *

* * *

In liberation, everything changes and nothing changes.

Everything changes because it's no longer 'your' life, and it's now seen in absolute clarity. Everything changes because it all becomes so wonderfully light and transparent. Everything changes because now life is no longer in opposition to death. Everything changes because everything you rejected, everything you denied, everything you pushed away is now seen to be nothing but an expression of unconditional love.

And yet, nothing changes. Chop wood and carry water. Eat, shit, grow old. Get cancer. Scream in pain in the middle of the night. None of that stops. This isn't about living in some New Age fantasy world. This isn't about taking on comforting concepts and surrounding yourself with cotton wool. This is reality at its most raw. Nothing can be blocked out anymore. It's the end of control. It's a free fall into an intimacy with everything. It's a love affair with what is. It's an absolute alignment with life.

* * *

this…

I'm walking through Brighton. There is
only this: kids screaming, bus engines
roaring, young lovers embracing, an old
lady hobbling towards me. Our eyes meet,
nobody looking at nobody. Nothing
between us. Only intimacy.

A homeless man asks for some spare
change. He is already home but does not
know it, although I do not tell him this.
A hand reaches into a pocket, and coins
are taken out.

A little red-faced toddler in blue
dungarees bumps into me. He looks up,
our eyes meet, and it's the old lady
again, and it's the homeless man.
Everyone is everywhere, and everyone is
nobody, walking through Brighton on this
beautiful sunny day.

I'm back in my flat, washing up. Now there
is only the chinking of plates, the
glistening of bubbles, the *splish-splash*
and the *drip-drip* and the *whoooosh* of
water as it shoots out of the tap. I watch
as the washing up does itself.

Now I'm having dinner with my mother and
father. They're debating politics and

religion over dessert. Voice, silence, voice, silence, and one is equal to the other. These eyes are entranced with the froth on top of a cup of coffee, glittering and sparkling in a shaft of sunlight. My parents' voices mingle with the froth, and the universe is nothing more than a frothy musical dessert full of old women and red-faced toddlers in blue dungarees, washing up and homeless people, screaming kids and roaring bus engines.

4

NONDUALITY: NOTHING TO GET, NOTHING TO DEFEND, NOTHING TO TEACH

Die and become.
Until you have learned this,
you are but a dull guest on this dark planet.

- Goethe

I have never had the sense that liberation has anything to do with me, with the character the world calls Jeff. I have never felt that I was in any way special.

In fact, that's exactly what fell away: the specialness of Jeff. Yes, the shocking realisation was that the freedom I'd been seeking for a lifetime turned out to have nothing to do with me at all! Nothing to do with anything I'd ever done, or not done. Nothing to do with effort or attainment or adding anything to the seeker. No, no, no. The seeker was *destroyed*, once and for all.

And so there is nothing to defend. I don't write and talk in order to prove that my take on nonduality is the 'correct' one, whatever that would mean. There is no need to make any claims, boasts or promises about my communication of this message, since I've never, ever, seen it as mine. There is no need to compare and contrast this expression with any other. There is no need to condemn teachers who aren't quite as 'nondualistic' or 'awakened' as me, whatever the hell any of that would mean. It's not a competition. It's not a war. It's unconditional love, and I don't own it. And even if I could own it, I wouldn't want to. It's too precious.

And with that I think, comes a certain humility. If there is any 'hallmark' of liberation – or whatever you want to call it – perhaps it's that. I can only speak from experience. You see, Jeff is constantly *humbled* by the wonder of what is, by the grace of this divine, purposeless, priceless play. And he knows that his words are always and forever equal to the barking of a dog or the miaowing of a cat. They are simply part of the song of Being, the divine dance of nothing and everything which reveals itself in and as everything and nothing, which sings and shines from the toothbrush as I brush my teeth in the morning, from the fish and chips that I munch on the beach, from the cold autumn breeze as it lovingly caresses my cheek, from the dog shit that I step in on the way home, ruining my new shoes.

Life happens, but there is nobody there to whom it happens. And when there is nobody there, there is nobody there who could ever become defensive, possessive or even smug about their own understanding or expression of this. There is nobody there who could ever believe their own bullshit anymore. Nobody there who could possibly care about what the world thinks, or doesn't think, of them or their 'message'.

Nothing to defend – that goes right to the very heart of this communication.

* * *

To the individual, this freedom, this grace, will always seem out of reach.

The moment you have an individual, you have separation, and the moment you have separation you have the longing to end that separation, to heal the divide, to come home. It's the wave longing to return to the ocean. And of course on some level the wave *knows* that it was never for one moment separate from the ocean – that the sense of being a wave is merely a temporary contraction of the whole.

The little wave is inherently a seeker, and he runs around the world like a headless chicken, trying to find something which of course he never lost in the first place. And he never lost this because he never had it. He always *was* it. The wave was always, always, a perfect expression of that which cannot be expressed. You – the character, the person, the individual – were always the divine expression, expressing itself perfectly, completely, and exhausting itself in that expression, leaving no trace, no residue.

And the cosmic joke? Even the individual's endless and exhausting search to come home – even that was always the divine expression. It was always Oneness seeking itself.

Well, of course it was. There is only Oneness.

And so when the search collapses, what collapses along with it is the sense of being an individual separate from the whole, the sense of being a little wave in a big ocean. It's not an intellectual thing. It's a collapse into Intimacy. Totally beyond the intellect. Totally beyond words.

But here's the rub: it's not something that you could ever have, or do.

Why?

Because you are looking for this in all the wrong places, and all your doing is directed towards a future that will never arrive. You are looking for this within the world. That is to say, you are looking for it within your world. And there is no other.

* * *

You see, the character and the character's world are inseparable. Once you have a character, you immediately have a world in which that character functions. A world in which that character lives and breathes and sees himself. An angry character sees an angry world. A depressed character sees a depressing world. A spiritual seeker sees a world full of things to look for, a world full of teachers and teachings and the hope and promise of salvation.

The seeker only ever sees his own world.

And within that world, the seeker hears about awakening or liberation or whatever you want to call it. And he begins to look for it within his world.

Anything is possible within the seeker's world. Within the seeker's world there are a million different spiritual paths and processes and practices and goals. A million things to do, a million things on offer. Within the seeker's world, you can look for enlightenment, you can wait for liberation, you can anticipate some sort of energetic transformation. Within the seeker's world, you can go to meetings and hear about future events that might or might not happen to you. It's a world full of belief. It's a world full of second-hand concepts passed down by well-meaning people who really believe what they tell you.

But liberation is not something that the seeker could ever find in his world, because it is *the dissolution of the seeker and, along with it, his world.* It's a falling-away of seeker and world, and a plunge into something much more mysterious, vibrant, and alive than those second-hand concepts ever promised.

And that plunge, well, the moment we talk about it, we are back into the language of seeker and world. But of course that's the only language we have. All teachings function within this realm of seeker and world (taken together, we could call this the 'dream world'). Even these words, and the words spoken in my meetings, function within the dream world, and that is why, as I always say, I know that the moment I speak about this, it's simply not true. The moment I speak about this, I've made it into something, something in the dream world, something for the seeker to hold onto and attempt to understand. I've turned it into something for you to get in the future.

In a sense, if you want to talk about nonduality you're doomed from the beginning. That's part of the humility too: the seeing that you will never be able to express this. And that even the idea of a 'perfect' nondualistic communication −if that were even possible−is still totally and completely within the dream world.

* * *

In this dream world, everything is in perfect balance. A depressed character is met with a depressing world, wherever he goes. A fearful character is met with a terrifying world, wherever he goes. A seeker is always met with teachers who will cater to the seeking, feed the seeking.

In fact, the teacher needs the student as much as the student needs the teacher. The student functions in the teacher's world in the same way as the teacher functions in the student's world. He meets a need. Because of course, a teacher cannot know himself as a teacher unless he, in some way, uses the students to create and maintain that identification. And so he clings to them as tightly as they cling to him.

In the dream world, in your quest to be a person, to be a somebody rather than a nobody, in your attempt to make your life work, you always meet your own reflection.

And the teachers promise you so much! They promise a future event called enlightenment, or awakening, or some sort of shift or change in perception that you can or cannot obtain.

But in the falling away of the self-contraction and along with it, the contracted world space in which all teachers and teachings operate, the grace is revealed, and it has nothing to do with any sort of future event, or spiritual experience, or shift in perception, or transformation of consciousness, or anything else that was promised by the dream teachers. And it's shockingly ordinary. It's drinking a cup of tea. It's eating fish and chips. Except now, nobody drinks the tea, and nobody eats the fish and chips. Drinking tea just happens. Eating fish and chips just happens. Tea drinks itself. Fish and chips eat themselves. That's about as close as we can get in language.

It's totally beyond anything you expected. And it's not something new that appears—it's a revelation of something that was already there, apparently hidden but really always in plain view. This ordinary life has always been longing to reveal its secrets. The fish and chips and the cup of tea—and yes, even the dog shit on the pavement—were always the Beloved calling us home.

This is not an intellectual realisation. If it were that simple, it would just be a matter of changing your thoughts, for example from "This isn't it" to "This is it", or from "I'm not awake" to "I am awake". Within the dream world, of course, changing thoughts can be a wonderful thing. If you're going to have a dream, it's probably better to have a happy dream! If you're going to have a dream, why not think positively instead of negatively! Why not think you're awake instead of asleep! Within the dream world, the individual can do a million different things to their thoughts, and thoughts in turn can create a million different experiences. But what we're talking about here is totally beyond all of that. It cannot be captured by any thought-created formula. In fact, "There is no person" and "There is a person" both miss the point. "There is choice" and "There is no choice" both miss the point. Within the dream world, these pairs of opposites arise together and fall away together. But they cannot take you to where you really want to go: your own absence.

* * *

Beyond the opposites of the self-contraction, this grace, this wonder constantly shines, and in fact it is only because of this grace that the self-contraction can appear to manifest at all. Being plays every role, even the role of the one who appears to be ignorant of Being. It's all Being. That is the revelation. For no-one.

The person was always imprisoned by their world, without ever realising it. And then they imagined that freedom could be found *within* that world! In the falling away of person and world, there is no person to be imprisoned, of course. There is just what is. Just nothing being everything. Just this – and even that is saying too much.

All we can really do is try to point back to this as clearly and as honestly as possible, using words to go beyond words. And in the dream world the arguments go on:

"My teacher/teaching is better than yours!"
"Teacher X is completely dualistic – she gives people a spiritual practice, which means that she still sees separate people!"
"Teacher Y teaches purely from the intellect!"
"Teacher Z still uses the word 'I' – he couldn't possibly be liberated!"

You wouldn't believe how often I hear this sort of thing.

In the dream world, some of those arguments may have some validity. But they all completely miss the point: *nobody* can teach this. There are no enlightened people, no awakened people. No person has ever reached liberation. Because there are no people at all. The person is the mirage. Nobody owns this freedom.

And that's the beauty of this, that's the joy of it: what we're talking about is totally free, constantly available, always and forever offering itself unconditionally. And when this message is really heard, when the seeking dissolves and the self-contraction heals, what these words are pointing to is revealed in absolute clarity, and the my-teaching-or-teacher-is-better-than-yours game that gets so very serious and tedious is seen to be what it always was: an intellectual game, a battle of egos, a distraction from what, for this character anyway, has always been at the very core this message: unconditional love, and the revelation and expression of that.

And all the while, beyond the futile attempts of the

character to communicate this message and defend that communication, this intimacy which is beyond measure and yet so totally ordinary lies quietly in the background, whispering so very softly that all is well, and that, of course, there is "nothing to defend... nothing to defend..."

this...

An old couple walk at a snail's pace towards the taxi rank at Brighton station. The woman is on crutches, the man is tiny and hunched over and walks a few paces in front of her. He looks at the ground as he walks. He can't look up; his bent spine won't allow it. These eyes lock onto him. Breathing stops. I am seeing myself. Love hobbles towards the taxi rank at Brighton station, and love watches in silence. More than anything in the world, I want this little hunched-over old man and his wife to arrive safely at the taxi rank, and I don't know why. Then, without warning, the head turns and it is all forgotten as new sounds and images flood in: a man talking loudly on a mobile phone, the smell of Cornish pasties, a half-naked lady advertising perfume on a billboard.

In a London Underground station a man lifts his daughter onto his shoulders as they queue up for the escalator. A voice booms over the loudspeaker: "WOULD THE MAN WITH THE GIRL ON HIS SHOULDERS PLEASE PUT HER DOWN? IT'S DANGEROUS TO CARRY CHILDREN ON THE ESCALATORS!" The world stops. It is love that lifts its daughter onto its shoulders, and it is love that warns a father of danger. Love is talking to itself. I am the voice on the loudspeaker, warning myself not to hurt myself. I am the father who loves his daughter more than life itself. Tears trickle down my face, smear onto the dirty floor of Victoria station, and are immediately wiped out.

The hunched-over old man and his wife reach the taxi rank, the father puts his daughter down and holds her hand as they descend the escalator, and I find myself at Burger King being served by a young girl who places fries and a burger on a red tray, looks up at me and asks "Would you like any ketchup with that?"

"Yes please," I reply.

An unwashed homeless man who stinks of beer and body odour picks his nose and eats it and looks at me, then comes right up close and says "What the fuck are you looking at, mate?"

And how damn *perfect* it all is when you are dead and it no longer matters what happens.

5
THE ORIGIN OF THE WORLD

The world exists only when we think about it;
creation stories are for children.
In reality the world is created every moment.

- Jean Klein

You really have no way of knowing what *this* is.

You really have no way of knowing who you are. Or what you are. Or where you are. Until thought comes into the picture and says 'I'.

'I'
'I am'
'I am... a person'
'I am... a person... sitting in a room...'

Before thought tells the story of what is, there is only the Mystery of it all. Prior to the story, there is only the not-knowing.

Prior to the 'I' there is no world. This is where everything begins.

* * *

Present sights, sounds, smells. Feelings in the body happening. Thoughts arising out of nowhere. The sound of the rain falling outside. Hunger in the belly. A dog barking. The television blaring. This is all there is.

What is given in this moment is already a perfect expression of life. Life expresses itself totally right here, and hides nothing from view. Nothing is absent here. And of course, before you can even call it a 'moment', it's already gone.

At the heart of this present appearance, at the heart of this astounding show of sights and sounds and smells, there is no person, no centre, no reference point, no puppeteer pulling on the strings. The lights are on, but nobody is home. There are sounds, feelings, thoughts, but there is simply no person there hearing the sounds, feeling the feelings, thinking the thoughts. Life is not happening *to* anyone or *for* anyone—it's just happening. It's happening for no-one.

Your absence is identical with the presence of the world.

And that's why we can say that life is already liberated. Life is already free from the personal self, and so it's already completely free to be exactly what it is, to be itself perfectly. Indeed, from the very beginning it has been liberated. It was never bound, so the search for freedom was always in vain.

Liberation has nothing to do with an individual. It's not something that you could ever get. It's not something that some people have and others don't. It's not a state, not an experience. It's not something that happens in time. It's not mine and it cannot be yours. It's not a thing. It's nothing and it's everything. If there is liberation, it's for nobody.

You could never find this in a book, and no teacher can teach you this. Nobody can give this to you. And even if they could, how could they have prepared you for *this*? For what's happening now, in *this* moment? No, nobody could have told you about *this* present appearance, the one that's happening right now. *This* is always completely new, totally fresh. It could never have been predicted.

And the wonderful thing about this appearance is that it's always yours and yours alone, although there is no 'you'. It's absolute intimacy, for no-one. Again, words will never touch it.

* * *

Being is already being everything, perfectly. It's playing all the roles. The carpet, the ceiling, the walls, the windows. Yes, it's there even in the lowest things, in the smallest things, in the most insignificant things.

Any idea the individual has about liberation will be destroyed by this aliveness. This aliveness will just burn up any ideas you have about it. In a sense, this aliveness is very destructive. It's always burning up the old concepts, the outdated ideas. Every single carry-over from the past is always being blown away by what's happening. By the sound of the heart beating, of breathing. By the walls and by the carpet. By present sights, sounds and smells.

Life is always calling you back to itself. Everything is calling you back to this. And everything says: listen, see, for you are hearing nothing but God, you are seeing nothing but the divine expression.

* * *

It can be incredibly challenging when you first hear this message. It's shocking to hear that you are nothing. And yet it's only because you are nothing that anything has ever happened at all. It's only because you are nothing that the sound of the rain outside can be heard presently. Nothing is blocking it out. It's only because you are nothing that these words can be read right now.

121

Nothing is blocking them out. It's only because you are totally absent that this presence can be revealed at all. It's only because you are *not* that everything *is*. You allow the world to be.

Everything that happens is always pointing to your absence. It's pointing to the death of everything that's gone before, the death of the old, the death of the known. The death of who you thought you were. The death of what you thought you needed. What you thought you wanted.

* * *

People sometimes react with anger and fear when they hear this message for the first time. They are shocked to hear that the character they take themselves to be may be nothing more than a fantasy. "I'm nothing? I thought I was everything! I thought I did everything!" Yes, this goes against everything we ever thought or believed. It can be very challenging to hear.

But here's the thing: when you are nothing, when you have nothing, when all there is is presence, what's left is an astonishing openness to everything. To sensations, to feelings, to everything that life has to offer. What's seen is that the attempt to block out life only ever led to exhaustion, frustration and despair. The attempt to block out life didn't work. Because life will always prevail. It will destroy any attempts to block it out. It will burn up everything in its place. It is pure aliveness. It is raw energy. It cannot be blocked out. It won't stand for that.

In a sense, liberation is a kind of loss. It's a loss of everything that wasn't necessary. A loss of all the bullshit. A seeing in clarity of what was already there, but what for a lifetime was ignored in the pursuit of something more.

It's a life lived without the seeking. It's the death of the seeker, and the beginning of something else.

When that search collapses, when the absolute futility of the seeking is seen in shocking clarity, then *this*– what is–becomes quite fascinating, because it's all that's left. Yes, you're stripped of everything, quite literally everything, and you stand naked in front of life, with no way to block it out anymore, totally exposed, totally vulnerable, but there's a strength there too, a strength that comes from the absolute certainty that no power in the world can touch you. You stand naked in front of life, and become it, and it's all over. ⚹

And then you become very intimate with what is. *What is* becomes your constant companion. It can never leave you. It's a love affair that goes on forever, and you can never, ever be lonely again.

* * *

Let's say it plain: the search failed. The mind failed to get what it wanted. It was always looking for something, something to get in the future, and that future never came. ⚹

The search failed and it was *bound* to fail. It was built upon a faulty premise: that there was a person here. A person who felt incomplete and wanted to put an end to the sense of being incomplete. When it is seen that there's nobody here, that search crumbles to the ground.

And so the search fails, fails absolutely, and you're left sitting here, in a room, on a chair. That's it. Sitting here. Ordinary room. Ordinary chair. Hunger in the belly. Present sounds. Smells of food cooking. A fly buzzing over there. And what a massive disappointment this is, to a mind that was expecting so much more! "We've failed miserably! We didn't get what we wanted! We didn't reach our goals!" And so we call this message 'hopeless' because it leaves us with just this, and we're still clinging onto the hope of a future salvation. We secretly still believe that a future salvation is possible! We look around and we say "This? This is nothing!" That's because we're waiting to get everything in the future.

 But when all hope is gone, really gone, the hopelessness goes too. You only feel hopeless when you're still clinging onto hope. Onto the hope that there is something more than this. But when all hope is gone, really gone, there is no way of being hopeless anymore. Hope and hopelessness dissolve, and you're left here, sitting on this chair, and you realise, "Wait a second – it's not all that bad. What's happening isn't all that bad. In fact, it's pretty wonderful! This chair is comfortable. Breathing is happening. The body is warm. In fact, there is nothing wrong with this moment at all!" And then there is the shocking realisation: maybe it's always been okay here.

You see, for a lifetime we made *this* into the enemy. *This* was never good enough. *This* was too ordinary, too dull. *This* was always a means to an end. We wanted the extraordinary. We didn't want *this* – we wanted to awaken from *this*. We didn't want *this* – we wanted a different world, a different state, a different experience.

We made *this* into the enemy. We made life into the enemy. What was happening was never good enough for us.

But actually when you really stop and look at it, and feel it, and touch it, and taste it, how innocent life is! It's not the enemy at all! Life is so innocent. The chair—all it's ever been doing is just sitting there, offering itself, whispering "Come, sit down, rest yourself, I'm here for you." And the carpet that you've never really noticed before, because you've been so busy looking into the future for an awakening—see how it just lies there, offering itself, whispering "Come, stand on me, I ask nothing of you." You didn't see the carpet because you wanted to get enlightened first. You wanted to be an enlightened person standing on the carpet! You were going to work on yourself for fifty years, or meditate your way to Nirvana before seeing the carpet. Or perhaps you were going to wait until you were 'fully present' before allowing yourself to see the carpet! It was all a postponement. It was all a movement away. It was a movement into a future that never came. But the carpet was always so innocent. It was always just sitting there offering itself.

Life was always happening here, but we were so busy moving away.

And we missed the ceiling too. We were too busy trying to change ourselves, transform ourselves, become someone or something else. Never mind the ceiling, we wanted to awaken under that ceiling! And all the while the ceiling has so very gently and softly been trying to remind you that there's no such thing, that you're kidding yourself, that *this* is all there is. All the while the ceiling was a secret expression of the divine. Yes, Oneness was always there, hidden in the ceiling, the carpet, the clothes, the breathing, in everything. It was always there but we were too damn busy trying to improve our fictional selves to notice.

We never really knew what we were trying to become, we just knew that this wasn't enough. And so we didn't bother with the chair because we thought we had a future. We didn't bother with the ceiling because we thought we had a future. We didn't bother with life, with this aliveness, because we thought we had a future. We bought into the spiritual search. We bought into the stories of enlightened beings. We bought into the teachings.

Somewhere along the line the world told you that you were a little 'person', a separate 'me' who had to make it, had to succeed, had to become someone, and you believed that. In your innocence, you believed it all. You just didn't know better at the time.

So now we can grow up. We can mature. We can see this for what it is: the miracle appearing right before our very eyes. As if by magic, it's here. And how innocent it all is! We were never separate from this innocence, not for one moment. All those years that we spent trying to end the separation, and now we discover that we were never separate in the first place! And that the chair was always calling us back to this, and the ceiling was always calling us back to this, and the carpet was always calling us back to this. They were always pointing back home.

We got so attached to our teachers – the ones who tried to tell us how to live because they believed that they had found the answers and wanted to pass on the good news – that we missed the utterly obvious: life itself was always trying to teach us, life itself was always the one and only teacher. We were so busy searching for that awakening experience, that bliss experience, those second-hand experiences we'd read about, that we missed *this* experience. So busy looking for the extraordinary experience that we missed the ordinary experience. So busy kidding ourselves that we were 'spiritual people' and therefore that we needed to hang around other 'spiritual people' that we missed the old lady on the road who's probably more aligned with life than anyone and doesn't even know what the words 'spiritual' or 'awakened' mean.

* * *

You're always seeing this for the last time. You're never guaranteed another moment. It's so precious, so fragile. It's always the last time you're going to see the chair, the last time you're going to see the ceiling, the last time you'll see the carpet. The last time you'll see your hands. The last breath. It's just arrogance to think that you have another day. Another moment. What arrogance! Why do we deserve another moment? Well, the beauty is that we don't deserve it, but we get it anyway. And that's grace. We don't deserve it but we get it anyway, until we don't.

My goodness, we've been such naughty children! We've done so many bad things in our lives! Felt so much anger towards others! Judged so much! We don't deserve this grace! And yet it's here. It's given.

This is unmerited. Unwarranted. A gift that is given in spite of what we've done. In spite of what we've achieved or haven't achieved, what we believe or don't believe. We are nothing and yet in this moment we are given everything. Everything we need. What arrogance to think that we deserve anything more! At the root of the entire spiritual search is arrogance, narcissism, ego. At its root is me, me, me. At its root is I, I, I. I deserve this! I deserve that!

So that's where it all begins: I. I want. I need. That 'I', that person, seems so solid, so real, and yet in deep dreamless sleep, it's simply not there. The person with his or her wants, goals, and needs, is simply not there. And so this whole search is founded upon emptiness. It has no foundations. It is a castle in the sky.

And before 'I', before 'I want, I need', there is nothing. Before 'I', there are no wants, no needs. It is complete. There is no lack. Before the search arises out of the void there is no lack.

The moment the search arises, there is lack. Then we turn to the world to end the sense of lack, and teachers appear. The teachers are a projection of our sense of lack.

And the teachers promise you something in the future. Something they have, something that you – if you're lucky or work hard enough – can have too. And all this does is fuel the sense of incompleteness, the sense of being a separate person who is 'not there yet'. And the teachers love this because if you are lost, and if they can show you the way, their sense of self is held in place and they are no longer threatened by the void.

We just can't seem to let go of our teachers, to stand alone without any authority and face life head-on, with no safety net. Because to let go of the teacher would mean also letting go of the student. Who would you be if you were no longer a student? To let go of the teacher, we must let go of our very selves. It's a death. For a lifetime perhaps we've defined ourselves based on our spiritual path, our practices, our teachers. We've seen ourselves as seekers. Who would we be without the seeking? Who would I be if I weren't a seeker anymore? That question can be a terrifying one.

That's why most people aren't interested in this message. They still want to be seekers. They want to live, they don't want to die. And that's fine, that's part of the play too. But for those who are ready to listen, what is being shared here is the possibility of letting go of the teacher, letting go of the path, letting go of the seeker, and standing alone without any crutches, without any reference points. The possibility of living without a map, without a guidebook. The possibility of living in free fall, of facing up to the rawness of experience without anyone there telling you what to feel, what to think, how to change. To be without mummy and daddy. Without your idea of God. Without heaven and hell. Without a world.

To be without a past, without a future, that's the freedom. To be utterly alone, but never for one moment lonely. To meet life head-on. To admit that you're simply exhausted from a lifetime of seeking, of pretending, of trying to avoid the rawness of experience. To see life in absolute clarity and know that it was always the miracle. To see that it was never your life in the first place.

And we call that 'death'. And we fear that. This is how insane the mind has become.

* * *

And so the whole thing ends in the absolute mystery of it all. It ends in wonder. It ends in gratitude. It ends in simplicity. It ends the way it began, in innocence. Jesus said "Unless you become like little children, you will not enter the Kingdom of Heaven", and this is what he was talking about.

You are left with only the mystery, and everything emerges from that and falls back into it. Where it all comes from, and where it's going, nobody knows. Anyone who claims to know is kidding you. The mystery cannot be known. Nobody knows.

It comes out of nothing and falls back into nothing, and there is this astonishing play in-between. This is nothing playing the game of being everything. Oneness playing the game of being separate. And we could never find the mystery, we could never reach awakening, because we were always already living it. We've always been living it.

And of course, *we've* not been living it at all—*it's* been living itself. *It's* been waking up in the morning, and brushing its teeth and going to work. And *it's* been doing the dishes, and going out with friends and coming home and getting into bed. *It's* been doing everything.

And there's always been something here that has quietly, gently, innocently watched as the character Jeff was born and grew up and lived his life, and will watch quietly, gently, innocently as Jeff gets old, gets ill and dies. It will watch with equanimity and love as the body ceases to function and falls away like an unwanted piece of clothing. This play will play itself out, and the character will live their life, and everything will be embraced by a love with no name.

It just doesn't matter anymore what happens to the character. It just doesn't matter anymore. So tomorrow Jeff gets knocked down by a bus. Okay, okay, I can take that. *This* has been enough.

The origin of the world is identical with its end.

And all that is left at the world's end is the most profound gratitude for what is given.

this...

I'm sitting in a Jeff Foster nonduality
meeting. A woman is asking a question.
She wants to experience Oneness; she is
looking for hints and tips. Her pen is
poised to take notes. The sound of her
voice mingles with warmth in the stomach,
a slight ache in the left foot, and the
vague smell of somebody's aftershave.
Someone to my left coughs and blows their
nose. A car beeps its horn. This place is
alive.

The woman's words are registered
somewhere. I hear only the melody of her
voice. Everything in the room is dancing
to the melody. The car, the man blowing
his nose, the child looking bored at the
back, they are all caught up in a secret
dance.

The woman sits down. She doesn't realise
that the sound of her voice has just
answered her question.

Silence. I have no answer for her. This
is empty of questions and answers. I am
a child, I know nothing about nonduality.
All I know is car horns, the whiff of
aftershave, the blowing of noses and
aching of feet. This is where I live.
Right here, not in some other dimension.

The mouth opens to speak, even though I have no idea what to say.

"Did you bring the sugar, darling?"

Amy and I are sitting on Brighton beach, looking out to sea and drinking tea out of paper cups. In silence, we cuddle and watch as the English Channel breathes in and out. A seagull waddles up to us, gives out a high-pitched screech, and shits onto the pebbles.

6

CONFESSIONS II

If you want answers, if you want to learn something, if you want to 'get' something, if you want to be comforted, go see a teacher.

If you are exhausted from the search, if you are prepared to lose everything, if you are ready to die and come home, then read on...

* * *

Sometimes people ask me very complicated questions about the nature of reality. Often it seems as though they are looking for something they cannot find. There is a desperation in their eyes. It's like a longing for something they cannot name.

If only they could see that the answer to their questions is right there, literally right there in the sound of their voices asking the questions.

Your voice is God singing. And so it doesn't really matter what the question is, because the answer is always the same.

* * *

* * *

All suffering is a variation on "This isn't enough".

When what's happening is enough,
there cannot be anything called suffering.

And look—what's happening is enough.
How do you know? It's happening.

* * *

There is no path that will get you any closer to this.

Nobody needs to teach you how to breathe. Nobody needs to teach you how to 'be'.

Being doesn't need you to practise 'being'. Being is already being itself perfectly. You don't need to add another layer to Being.

There's Being, and there's a person practising 'being'. And yet, the cosmic joke? The person who practises being is already 100% Being. It's Being practising itself. Being being itself, perfectly! But that is true whether you're practising being or having a pint of beer at the local pub. Nothing is more 'spiritual' than anything else. And that's going to be difficult to hear if you're very attached to your 'spiritual' persona.

* * *

You will never free yourself from the search. You *are* the search.

You are using seeking to get rid of seeking. Seeking the end of seeking is more seeking than ever. My goodness, it's like a dog chasing its own tail. No wonder this spiritual game can lead to so much confusion and frustration.

Consider the possibility that you are not reading these words.

* * *

The individual looks around the world and asks "What is the point of all this? What is the meaning of life?"

If there's any point to this manifestation, it's in the seeing of it. Everything is there to be seen.

It's like waking up from a dream, and wondering what the point of the dream was. Well, from within the dream, there could be a million different answers to that question. A million different meanings, explanations, theories.

But when you step out of the dream – and of course, that's not something that *you* can do – what's seen is that the dream was only ever leading to one place.

Within the dream of time and space, it seemed as though A was going to lead to B. In the waking up, it is seen that A was only ever leading to the waking up. And so it wasn't really 'leading' anywhere at all, because outside of the dream there is no time, and so no causation.

Everything in the dream points to the possibility of liberation.

* * *

* * *

Everything that's ever happened in your life has been utterly appropriate. Everything arose to meet the character exactly where he or she was. Well of course it did: everything that ever happened has been a projection of yourself.

It's all been utterly appropriate because it's all been pointing back *here*. Everything that ever happened has been pointing back to *this*. Right now, your life history is simply a story arising presently. No other story could possibly be arising now but that one. Again, it's like when you wake up from a dream, and you see that the dream *was the only dream you could have had*.

We've all been dreaming the 'correct dream'. People think that they need to alter their dream in order to reach something called liberation. But in liberation, it no longer matters what happened in the dream. Besides, attempting to change the dream would just be more dreaming.

* * *

To a person, life can seem serious. If you were born, and if you're going to die one day, and if you only have a certain amount of time to live before you die, then life is serious.

When all of that falls away, the seriousness goes with it. It becomes impossible to take anything too seriously. It becomes impossible to become too involved in the story of the world. And yet, for the sheer joy of it, you can play with the world. Although there is no 'me' and no world, like a child I play and pretend that there *is* a 'me' and there *is* a world.

And then I get a 'you' too, which is wonderful. And not just a 'you' but a 'him' and a 'her' and even a 'them'. Out of nothing, this astonishing dream world arises. And it's a dance, it's a play of light and sound, and it's all so very precious because it's all there is.

Yes, the seriousness goes out of it, the heaviness. I used to be so serious about something called spirituality! I used to be so heavy about something called nonduality! I used to get very upset when people didn't see what I saw! I used to get so very angry at all those unawakened people! I was so serious about something called freedom.

Life is light; it has no centre. There is no reference point. It's just playing. Play along with it. What else is there to do, when the seeking is no longer there?

* * *

* * *

You will never be fully *present*. If you were fully present, you would be destroyed. 'You' and presence cannot coexist.

We say "I am going to be present now". But we are trying to use time in order to reach presence. We are trying to use time to reach the timeless.

There is only presence; everything is already happening in total presence. Even the most elaborate and mesmerising thoughts about tomorrow and yesterday are happening in presence. The 'you' who is trying so hard to become present–this 'you' is already happening in presence!

In fact, 'you' cannot do anything, let alone become present! A story cannot *do* anything. A story is just a collection of thoughts, and a collection of thoughts has no power. But the mind doesn't want to hear this! It feels threatened by this message!

How wonderful to see how powerless you really are. How wonderful to give up and dissolve into the stunning effortlessness of this. To be crucified and die into eternal life. What a relief, not to have to *do* anything or *be* anyone anymore. Of course, you can still play at *doing* and *being*, but the seriousness goes out of it.

* * *

You want awakening? First of all find out if there's anybody sitting on this chair. When it's seen that nobody is sitting on this chair, it's also seen in clarity that there is nobody there who could ever become awakened.

* * *

The sound of rain falling outside. But who hears it? And where is 'outside'? Listen carefully. There is only that sound happening: *pitter patter pitter patter*. Only the sound, but where is the person who is listening? You will never find that person. You'll only ever find the *pitter patter pitter patter*. Just sounds happening.

And it's not happening 'outside' as opposed to 'inside'. It's happening right here, the only place where anything happens. Beyond outside or inside, beyond the opposites which define our lives, everything happens here. The rain, thoughts, wars, genocides, rock concerts, the solar system, pain, everything.

And then you come to see that really there is no 'here' either. 'Here' requires its opposite, 'there'.

When even that dichotomy falls away, all you're left with is... well, *pitter patter pitter patter*.

And perhaps not even that.

* * *

There is no such thing as silence. If you really listen to silence, you'll find that it simply brims with aliveness, with life. The silence is noise. The noise is silence. They are not two.

Our problem is that we want the silence and not the noise. We want a silent mind rather than a noisy one. It's like when we want to meditate in silence, but the little buzzing fly in the room is creating too much noise, and so our meditation is disturbed. So the fly is rejected.

It's the same with thoughts. We want nice, happy, spiritual, loving thoughts, but not the other kind. So if the other kind, the buzzing fly-type thoughts occur, there is the attempt to get rid of them. We are at war with ourselves. Mind is at war with mind.

When that war falls away, thoughts are just allowed to be there. Any thoughts. All thoughts. They all have a rightful place here. All the flies in the world can come, but because there is no longer any interest in moving towards something called 'silence', and rejecting something called 'noise', the flies can stay for as long as they like. That is love.

* * *

* * *

You cannot stop thinking. Did you start thinking? If you were doing the thinking, if you were creating the painful thoughts, you would be able to stop doing that. You would be able to stop right now, and you never would have started in the first place.

See? They're not yours. Just as the bird singing out there isn't yours, so that thought isn't yours. Birds sing, thoughts happen, end of story.

* * *

There could have been *nothing*. And yet there appears to be *something* here. There might have been a dark, empty void with nobody there to know it. And yet there appears to be something happening here. There appear to be sights, sounds, smells, colours, motion. Bodies, trees, flowers, cars. Wars, cancers, puppies. There could have been nothing, and yet there is something.

That's the only miracle. There's no need to make one movement away from that. We're always seeing the miracle unfolding right before our very eyes. Do we realise how lucky we are?

* * *

* * *

People ask "If everything is One, why does there appear to be separation?"

It's only a separate person who would ask that. The wave looks around at the ocean and asks "Why are there so many waves, if it's all ocean?"

But of course, there never was a separate wave. And so the questions dissolve and the answer becomes absolutely apparent.

* * *

Why does One seem to appear as two? Well, in actuality it doesn't. Oneness doesn't *appear* as anything. It *is* everything that appears.

Actually Oneness does nothing, because it is not separate from anything! We shouldn't really call it Oneness at all, but it's as good a word as any. We could drive ourselves mad arguing over words...

* * *

* * *

So many spiritual teachings are about bringing your awareness back to the present moment, paying attention to what is, allowing everything to be, or attempting somehow to be at peace with what's happening.

What I'm suggesting here, is that there is *only* what's happening, and nobody there who could pay attention, allow everything, or be at peace with what's happening. That would suggest separation from what's happening, and that is the primary illusion, which falls away in liberation. No, there are only present sights, sounds and smells, but nobody there who can be present or not.

"I'm present with what is" is just another *identity*.

When there's nobody there to be present, the idea of being present just becomes obsolete. And then there is only presence, and nobody there to know that.

* * *

* * *

Prior to the self-contraction, prior to 'I', there is no world. There is only awareness, with nobody there to be aware; only consciousness with nobody there who is conscious. Only Being, being itself perfectly, and totally unaware of itself, because prior to the 'I' there are not two, and it takes two for something to be aware of itself.

Prior to the 'I', there is absolutely nothing, and nobody there to know it as nothing. And every night, in deep dreamless sleep, as the self-contraction falls back into the ocean of Being, as the body heals itself after a day of contraction, there is a wholeness that the separate individual could never find.

And then, in the morning, the self-contraction happens. Being contracts to give the illusion of a separate wave in a vast ocean. And before you know it, you have a human being again. You have a person who looks out at a world and sees time, space, birth, death. You have an individual who on some level longs to be free from that individuality, and who will spend the rest of their days seeking that freedom in a million different ways.

And yet every night in deep dreamless sleep, that individual is obliterated. Something that seems so solid and real turns out to be nothing but a mirage. How tragic it all seems, when seen in contraction. And yet, when seen in clarity, how perfect it all is, how playful, how *light*.

* * *

There is a mirror. And suddenly, atoms and oceans and wars and supernovas and seagulls dance and play in front of the mirror, and are reflected. You watch the reflection: lovers embrace, a man gets cancer and dies in agony, someone else gives birth, someone else becomes a great actor or a great businessman, someone else finds a cure for cancer, someone else becomes a spiritual teacher, someone else loses all their money. And then, a moment later, the dance ends, and you look at the mirror, examine it up close, and you see that it is as clean, as innocent, as fresh as it was before the dance began. The mirror was not tainted by anything that happened.

And then you see that there is no way of separating the mirror from what was reflected in the mirror. The mirror was the reflection, and the reflection was the mirror. They are not-two.

And then you see that even the mirror isn't really there. And neither are you.

* * *

* * *

The intelligent person asks "If there is no 'me', and there is no 'you', why should there ever be compassion? Why shouldn't we just sit back and let the world suffer?" It's a very good question.

But this is the essence of compassion: that we are not two, that your pain is my pain, that your suffering is my suffering. It is only because we are not separate that there can be compassion at all. And so I see an old lady trying to cross the road, struggling with her heavy shopping bags, and although we're not separate, although there is no 'me' and no 'old lady', although it's all just a dream and her suffering is an illusion of mind, although we could sit here for years arguing over what is real and what is not, what I find is that this body moves, and it crosses the road, and it helps that old lady who does not and cannot exist for me.

Because of course, it's really helping itself. It sees itself as an old lady, and there is movement to help itself across the road. What else is there to do, when you are not? When there is nothing here to defend, there is only an openness to what happens.

And now, I find the feet moving across the road. Now, I find that they stay still. Now, it moves, and now, it doesn't. There's no way of knowing where it's going. It moves or it doesn't.

It doesn't seem to stagnate. It doesn't seem to sit back and say "It's all a dream so why bother? Nothing is real so what's the point?" No, it doesn't have any time for those rigid, second-hand concepts. It is fully alive. It responds to life and nothing else. All the intellectual arguments and debates in the world cannot touch the aliveness of it.

It moves to help that old lady, or not. It helps when it can, and doesn't when it can't. It's not coming from a rigid position of "I must be a good person, I must help old ladies across the road". No, it's not coming from any conceptual position. If it were coming from a conceptual position, its actions would be rigid, forced, and perhaps even inappropriate. It's possible that help is the last thing the old lady needs! If you're coming from a fixed position, from a set morality, from a list of rules and regulations handed down to you, you might start to force help upon someone when what they really need at that moment is to be left alone. Sometimes the most 'compassionate' thing to do is to walk away.

It responds to what's happening and its responses are always fresh and unknowable. And afterwards, there's no sense of being a good person, or a compassionate person, because it's so clear that no person was involved at all! There was simply a movement to help, or not. You cannot take credit for what you didn't do.

This is the essence of compassion: to disappear in favour of what's happening. To dissolve into the vast open space in which a whole cosmos can play itself out, a space which is not separate from that cosmos.

And so, once again, the whole thing ends in the mystery of it all. The mystery of helping old ladies across the road!

* * *

Nothing is permanent. This life is so astonishingly fragile, so beautifully transparent. What you have, you may lose. Those you love may die. Your most stunning achievements may be forgotten.

As the Buddhists have always said, at the root of all suffering is the attachment to what is fleeting. And so there may be the attempt to relinquish all attachments, in order to move into a state of non-attachment.

But that just becomes another attachment, perhaps the biggest of all: the attachment to non-attachment.

What happens when all attachments fall away?

* * *

At the heart of the crucifix, there is eternal life. At the heart of the most excruciating worldly suffering, in the midst of broken bones and shredded skin, right there was eternity. Jesus did not attempt to escape from the cross but went willingly to his death, because he knew that all the violence of the world could not destroy the Indestructible, could not shake the Unshakeable, could not touch the unborn, undying essence of Life itself.

* * *

* * *

The Buddha never became enlightened.

Jesus was not crucified.

How can this be?

A Zen koan for you!

*Hint: When there is nobody there, who can do anything,
let alone get enlightened or die on a cross?*

* * *

* * *

Death is not something to fear, because it's not 'something' at all.

Every night we die – we just don't realise it. Every night, the story of 'me' falls away. Past, present and future fall away. 'Me and my difficult problems, me and my achievements, me and my spiritual search, me and my uncertain future' – it all falls away.

In deep dreamless sleep, there is absolutely nothing, nothing at all, and nobody there to know it as nothing. In deep dreamless sleep, you are dead, no question.

Why do we fear death? Every night we get to practise!

And then we wake up in the morning and say "I had a good sleep last night." Of course, you didn't have a good sleep, because you weren't there. You weren't asleep at all! You don't sleep and you don't die.

But the illusion of continuity must go on. And so there is a *linking up*: "I am the same person I was yesterday. I am the one who went to sleep and I am the one who woke up. I am the one who was born, and I am the one who will die." In that *linking up*, we get the illusion of a person.

* * *

Nobody has ever died.

Right now, there is only presence. A few moments before what we call death, there is only presence. Upon what we call death, there is only presence. What falls away is the person. What falls away is the person who splits life from death, the person who loves one and fears the other. What falls away is everything that can fall away. And what is left, there is no way of knowing. Anything we say about that would be purely conceptual.

And so death is a plunge into the unknown, the unknowable, the unborn, the undying. And even that is to say too much. Even that is just the person talking. In the absence of the person, there is nothing. No world. No birth. No death. No time. No space. No world in which to die, and no person to do the dying. *At the moment of death, what falls away is the person who could die.*

Nobody has ever experienced death. We only ever experience what we know. Death is what we know about death. When nothing is known, there can be no experience, and no death.

You think you are going to die? Find out if you were born first.

* * *

* * *

The woman who lives in fear secretly doesn't want to be free from fear; she wants to be free from 'the woman who lives in fear'.

The man dying of cancer secretly doesn't want to be free from cancer; he wants to be free from 'the man dying of cancer'.

The seeker secretly doesn't want awakening or enlightenment; he wants to be free from the seeker.

* * *

* * *

What you fear more than anything is your own absence.

And yet, your own absence is
what you long for more than anything.

But your absence is not something
that 'you' could ever experience.

That is why there is no death.

* * *

The great discovery:

Life does not need 'you'.

* * *

* * *

I'm lying in bed. The doctors have told me that I have a large abscess growing inside my bottom, and I'm waiting to have it removed. There is a searing, stabbing pain down below. I nearly pass out from the pain.

How astonishing to know that the present sensation of pain is *this* too. When I was a spiritual seeker, I wanted to be free from all pain and suffering and reach some elusive state called 'enlightenment' that I'd heard the masters and gurus talk about. I didn't want the pain, I wanted freedom from the pain!

What I couldn't see then is that it was exactly my search for freedom from pain that was creating the pain. Pain and 'freedom from pain' always go together, in the same way that black and white, up and down, absence and presence, subject and object always go together. The opposites create and maintain each other. My search for an escape from pain was nothing but a rejection of pain, disguised as some sort of noble, worthy, 'spiritual' pursuit. My search for enlightenment 'out there' was a rejection of what was happening here.

Pain had become the enemy. *What is* had become the enemy.

These days, in the absence of seeking, what is seen is that every present sensation is welcome here. Even pain is part of this. And really it is no longer possible to call it 'pain'. I have no idea *what* this is. Passing sensations, moment by moment, but nothing solid there called pain. And everything arises and dissolves in the barest empti-

159

ness, leaving no residue. That pain a moment ago, where is it? It's always gone. Pain is always the story of pain. It's always a story about a past.

It's like there's pain – if we had to give it a name – but there's nobody here who is *in* pain. There's just pain happening. Just pain happening now, or not. That's it. It's so astonishingly simple.

And don't get me wrong, the pain is painful! And sometimes, when the pain is intense, Jeff can curse and moan. But the cursing and moaning goes no deeper than the surface. Finally, after a lifetime of rejection, the pain is allowed to be itself.

Liberation is very raw. There is nobody here who could block anything out, who could reject any aspect of experience. So the pain is very raw, very alive. All defences fall away, and there is just the present appearance of everything, in its rawest and most honest form.

Pain is happening for no-one. It sounds like a complete paradox when you say it. Pain must be happening to *someone*, right? I mean, who else would call it pain but a *person*? That is why this will never be captured in words. There's pain, but because there's nobody here, there's no pain. Pain is there, and yet it's not there. Pain is absent, and yet who could deny that stabbing sensation between the legs?

And so the whole thing ends once again in the mystery of it all. The whole thing ends in the not knowing. There is just that mysterious sensation that the world calls 'pain' and rejects.

'Pain'. The moment we say it, it sounds like it's *there*. Like it's solid, like it's real. 'Pain', the word, cannot touch the aliveness of what's happening. What's happening will always remain totally liberated, and the words are always an afterthought.

Now, where did I put those painkillers?

* * *

* * *

We are afraid of being in too much pain. But there is no such thing as *too much* pain. There is exactly the amount of pain that there is in the moment.

There is this sensation of pain, happening now, and that's all there is. The rest is a story.

"It's too much for me! I can't take it! It will kill me! What did I do to deserve this?" All stories. The body has its own infinite intelligence. When the pain is really too much, when it really cannot cope any longer, it shuts down. It passes out or it ceases to function completely.

Left alone, the body takes care of itself. It would even cease to function, in order to spare you from being in *too much* pain. There is only benevolence.

* * *

* * *

"You say there's nothing that we can do to reach liberation, and yet you write books and give talks. Aren't you implying that there is something we can do, namely read your books and go to your talks? You say that we shouldn't listen to teachers, and yet you appear to be a teacher yourself. If, as you say, this cannot be put into words, why do you bother to talk and write books about it? Perhaps you secretly believe that you can teach this to people? Or perhaps you're just doing it for the money or the attention? Either way, haven't you fallen into the 'guru trap'?"

I get questions like this all of the time! My response is usually this: that we could find a million different reasons why we shouldn't ever speak about nonduality.

And yet, as I always say, why not. When the 'why' goes, life is lived out of the 'why not'. Silence and noise become equal. Not speaking about this and speaking about this become equal. It speaks, or it doesn't. Often it keeps quiet about this. When someone asks a question, sometimes it likes to offer a reply. Sometimes it sits down at a computer and starts typing and books start to take shape. Where the words come from, I don't know.

From the moment I started writing and talking about nonduality, I knew full well that I'd be accused of falling into the guru trap. That my words would be completely misunderstood, that I'd be accused of trying to sell shoddy goods, that I'd be labelled a wannabe guru, that I'd be compared to the other teachers and non-teachers out there. It was absolutely inevitable.

You know, for a long time I wasn't going to talk about this. I was going to keep quiet about it for the rest of my life. What had been seen here is that *this* is the miracle, that there is nothing higher or more sacred than what's happening, nothing more 'spiritual' than this present appearance. What had been seen is that there is an intimacy here that will never be communicated.

So, how to put this intimacy, this presence into words? Into the words of the world? Into the words of duality? I knew that the moment I uttered the first word about this, it wouldn't capture it at all. I knew that anything I said about this would not be true. *The Tao that can be told is not the Eternal Tao.* Words felt so dead in the face of this aliveness.

Besides, I had no interest in converting anyone, no interest in helping anyone to see this (after all, *who* would see it?), no interest in being someone special. How could I possibly be special? How could I ever separate myself from others and call myself 'special'? But I knew that the moment I started talking about this, it might make Jeff seem special. And yet, what went right to the core of this seeing is that Jeff was not special at all! No more special than the chair or the carpet! It was all the divine expression! The moment Jeff opened his mouth to talk about something called nonduality, it was inevitable that others would make him into something, or think that he had an agenda, or that he was doing it for the money, for the attention, for the fame. That he wanted to be a guru. It was inevitable that these projections would happen. I saw that from the very beginning, and that's why I was never going to speak about this.

And then, at some point, there was an invitation to talk,

and the mouth said "Yes". Previously it had said "No", and now it was saying "Yes". No and yes – totally equal in the seeing of this. So a while later, Jeff found himself in front of a small group of people, and the words started to come out. Still no sense that 'I' was speaking, still no sense that there was anything to say. Still no agenda, still just words happening or not. Whether 'other people' were listening or not, the seeing was the same. And although the crowds are a little bigger now, nothing has really changed at all. It's still a sharing with friends, and although at many of the meetings Jeff sits in front of an audience and talks, and questions are asked and he appears to reply, of course the secret is this: it's only Oneness meeting itself, and no teaching is happening at all.

But hey, the world will tell its stories. Until the seeker dissolves, and along with it the contracted self-sense, there will appear to be a world of teachers and teachings and gurus and lineages, and those projections will continue to be made. The seeker always sees a world of seeking. When all those projections fall away, what is seen in shocking clarity is that there cannot be any gurus, teachers, or teachings, because there cannot be any people at all. Wholeness is already here, and it has nothing to do with a separate person. What's seen is that we are already home, and the relief is absolute.

And so the world will think what it wants to about Jeff. He's doing it for the money? He's on an ego-trip? He's a nonduality missionary? He secretly sees himself as a guru? I can't make any of those stories mean anything anymore. I just go back to my very ordinary life by the sea in Brighton, have a cup of tea, and forget it all. I've always seen this as a sharing, between friends. And the sharing will go on until it doesn't. It's that simple. It comes from love and returns to love, as everything does.

A guru is someone who seriously believes that they can help you in your search for enlightenment or awakening. How ridiculous. The dream 'enlightenment' that the gurus promise is an experience in time, and there is no time. It's a construct of the mind, and there isn't one. It is an awakening for a person, and there is no person. Because the guru still sees you as a person who needs help (and still sees himself as a person who can give it) he keeps you locked in the illusion that you really are a person, and that there really is something called enlightenment. In his innocence, he keeps you trapped in the world of time and space.

When all of that falls away, what is seen is that there are no people to help, and no people who could ever awaken. In that, the guru-disciple or student-teacher relationship is obliterated. There were never any teachers, gurus, students or disciples: there was only ever unconditional love.

So, do what you do, and let the world say what they want about you. Let them crucify you if that makes them feel better about themselves. They are only crucifying their story of you anyway, in their dream world. They can destroy everything, literally every thing that exists, but they will never touch this aliveness, they will never taint this presence, they will never make even a little dent on Life.

I have no interest in what the world calls me. And for the sheer joy of it, I'll share this message until I don't. People will listen, or they will walk away, and it's fine either way.

And right now, as I sip my cup of tea, and watch the seagulls on Brighton Pier, none of it matters in the slightest. I laugh at the idea that I'm a teacher or guru. I'm nothing. The tea and the seagulls are everything. My nothing is the world's everything, and it all ends here, in absolute simplicity, and there is only love for all of it.

Just this, just this, forever and always.

* * *

* * *

I'm not telling you to give up your spiritual practices; giving up happens or it doesn't. Spiritual practices happen or they don't.

And remember:

Giving up on spiritual practices just becomes another spiritual practice.

The *anti-spiritual practice* ideology is just another ideology.

* * *

* * *

Watch out, the mind will turn everything in this book into just another goal. There is no person? *I want that!* The end of seeking? *I want that!*

And if you're not careful you'll start actually believing me when I say things like "I'm not here." It's not a concept to be believed. It's a string of words that are attempting to point to something that is totally beyond words. Once it turns into a belief, a concept, in a sense it's no longer true.

The person who really believes that they are 'not there'—and uses that belief to separate themselves from you—is living with a picture, a very personal image of themselves not being there. Think about it.

Yesterday's 'awakening experience' so easily becomes today's ego-trip.

* * *

An Advaita teacher once told me that he had a 'sense' that I was 'still there'. He felt that I was 'still a person', or that my person hadn't fallen away yet, or something like that. He of course was no longer a person. His 'person' had fallen away, apparently giving him the magic ability to sense when another, er... person's person hadn't yet, er... de-personalised itself.

Anyway, it all became very personal for someone who claimed that there was no person there.

What this personal non-person person was missing was that it's only a person that could see or sense the presence or absence of another person. It's all a game of projection and introjection. Smoke and mirrors. It's the person *here* who projects a person *out there*.

When there's really nobody *here*, there cannot possibly be anybody *out there* either. When that projection is no longer happening, there is no way of saying "I'm not here but you're still there." That would cease to make any sense whatsoever.

"I'm not here but you're still there" is just more separation. In liberation, it all falls away.

* * *

Anger is never yours. Once it becomes 'my' anger there's no end to it. Once it's 'my' anger it gets directed out at a world. "He made me angry! He's going to pay for that!" This is violence. This is war. This is suffering. My anger versus the world.

But it's never really *your* anger. It's just anger happening. And when there's nobody there manipulating anger, rejecting anger, trying to accept anger, transcend anger, or love anger; when there's nobody there attempting to forge an identity, nobody there using anger to get a better sense of who they are; when there is just anger happening and nobody there to whom it is happening, the anger just fizzles away in its own time. It lives its little life and fizzles away. It's not projected out into the world, or introjected back into something called a self, and so there is no problem with it at all. It's just an expression of energy. It becomes part of the texture of this moment. A bird sings over there, a car whooshes past over there, anger happens, and a little cat comes and rubs itself on your leg. Anger is just something else that's happening.

Anger – or fear, or any emotion, sensation or feeling – has its rightful place here. So often, spirituality becomes about getting rid of anger, getting rid of so-called 'negative' emotions and attempting to move towards something called the 'positive'. But this is a false dichotomy. This splits the world in two. This is an act of violence, and only violence can come from violence. Once that primal split has occurred there's no end to it. No wonder humans have killed so many humans over time. No, reality is whole, unified, unbroken. And what becomes shockingly apparent is that even anger is quite innocent, when seen in clarity. And then it doesn't need to be directed out at the world. Then it doesn't go and kill, maim or torture. Because what's seen is that there is nothing to defend here. There's just anger happening. It's nobody's anger.

When anger is just allowed to live its own little life, there is simply no problem. Anger just comes and goes. Fear, sadness, joy–they just come and go. They come and go and leave no trace. You cannot even say "I was angry" or "I was afraid". The moment you say it, the anger has gone, the fear has gone, everything has gone and something new has come to replace it. Everything is wiped clean and there is a return to innocence.

* * *

Why do we look for God when he is always staring us in the face? In every sight, sound and smell. In the trees and flowers and birds, in the roaring of traffic, in the beating of the heart. In these words and outside of them. In the white of the paper and the black of the ink. In the space and in the silence. In the in-between and the unseen as much as in the visible. In the throb of life and in the peace of death. In the cry of the baby, and the death rattle of the old man. In everything, as everything, God sings.

The word 'universe' literally means 'one song'.

this...

I am at a funeral. My aunt is being
lowered into the ground. People dressed
in black sniff and wipe their eyes.
Images of my aunt arise, living images,
images that are fully alive, images that
dance and sing. These are not *memories*
of my aunt. This *is* my aunt, and she is
alive. Great joy arises.

My stomach rumbles. I haven't eaten since
breakfast. A man walks up to me and says
he's sorry for my loss. Loss? Mine? What
have I lost? Nothing is lost here. Still,
I find myself smiling and saying thank you
and *meaning* it.

The people dressed in black begin a
collective moan. They are praying to their
God. Their cries mix with the splish-
splash of raindrops, the roar of traffic,
and the creak and thud as an empty coffin
hits the side of an empty grave. Nobody
is being buried, nobody prays for the
dead.

I feel the urge to urinate. I find myself
in the gents toilet. Some words scribbled
on the hand dryer: 'Press button, receive
bacon.' A great laughter wells up from
nowhere and obliterates the funeral. If
there is any death, it is this.

Back home, and Amy comes into the room. For a moment I don't recognise her. We embrace for the first time. For no reason, we start dancing, half-naked, to Stevie Nicks. *"Just like a white-winged dove, sings a song sounds like she's singing, ooh, ooh, ooh."* In total stillness, our bodies go wild.

Later on, I am watching a trashy home makeover TV show. An old woman comes home to find her living room has been transformed. Oh, the look on her face! Tears gush out like a waterfall.

7

THE OTHER SIDE OF NOTHING

In the beginning, trees were trees,
mountains were mountains,
and rivers were rivers.
Then came a time when trees were no longer trees,
mountains were no longer mountains,
and rivers were no longer rivers.
Now, trees are once again trees,
mountains are once again mountains,
and rivers are once again rivers.

- Zen saying

Let me tell you a little story.

In the beginning, trees were trees, mountains were mountains, and rivers were rivers. I was an ordinary person living an ordinary life.

Then in my mid-twenties, following a deep depression that nearly drove me to suicide, I became a very serious spiritual seeker. I became hooked on the idea of spiritual enlightenment and saw it as the ultimate escape from a world full of suffering and ignorance.

The world of form had become too much for me: I wanted to escape into the emptiness behind the world and live there. I wanted to get rid of Jeff and all his problems and dwell in the Absolute along with my friend the Buddha. I saw so clearly the problems of existence: the impermanence of everything, the inevitability of death, the illusory nature of the self, the empty nature of all phenomena; and my response to this was to detach myself from the world.

But I went too far, and fell into the Void. I detached myself so much that the world no longer mattered to me at all. I became trapped in nothingness. Trees were no longer trees, mountains were no longer mountains, and rivers were no longer rivers. Nothing had a name anymore. Life became cold and joyless. There was no me. No you. No self. No other. No world. No past. No path. No future. No love. No life. No meaning.

For days on end, I would walk aimlessly around Oxford, and there was absolutely nothing in existence, absolutely nothing happening at all. There was no world, no memory, nothing. There was only the Void.

I remember sitting for timeless eternities on park benches. Entire weekends would pass in the blink of an eye. The sun would rise and set, the rain would fall and stop falling, faces and voices would appear and disappear in the same moment, and I experienced none of it. Only the void was real, only nothingness. The world had ceased to exist for me. *And I thought that I was enlightened!* In *Steppenwolf,* Herman Hesse put words to my experience:

> *I found neither home nor company, nothing but a seat from which to view a stage where strange people played strange parts... Time and the world, money and power belong to the small people and the shallow people. To the rest, to the* real men, *belongs nothing.*

I believed that I was a *real man,* not one of those ignorant fools who were still lost in the 'relative' world, those unspiritual people who were ignorant of their 'true nature'. Back then, I thought that this was what nonduality was all about. I thought that nonduality was about detaching yourself from life and dwelling in the emptiness.

But what I could not see then was that the absolute detachment from life was totally dualistic. It takes a *person* to be detached, and a *world* to be detached from. Of course, after a lifetime of suffering it had initially been a relief to find the emptiness and escape from the hell that my life had become. But the emptiness had become another trap.

What I completely missed, at the time, was that emptiness is total fullness. I abided in emptiness, but there was still a 'me' doing the abiding. The emptiness had not yet collapsed into fullness. I hadn't died yet. I hadn't fallen in love with everything yet. That's where it all was heading.

* * *

Finally, the detachment collapsed. Everything does eventually. Finally, there was the death of the person, the person who could be detached or not, and a revelation, for no-one, that *this is it*. The joylessness fell away, and there was a plunge into the absolute mystery of it all.... totally beyond words, totally beyond language.

For so long there had been a deadness. For so long I'd sat back and watched the world go by without me. The world had become the enemy, because it wasn't essentially real. Everyday human interactions had lost their meaning, because there were no others. It had been such a *denial* of the relative, a *denial* of the world. There was still a 'me' there, denying life. Pretending he was more 'spiritual' or 'awakened' than others, feeling smug and safe and somewhat arrogant, but secretly joyless in his emptiness.

The freedom I'd initially found in the emptiness had morphed into a prison. Freedom in the formless had become a denial of form. But, as the Buddhist Heart Sutra has been reminding us for thousands of years:

Form is emptiness and the very emptiness is form; emptiness does not differ from form, form does not differ from emptiness; whatever is form, that is emptiness, whatever is emptiness, that is form.

181

* * *

And then it all collapsed. The denial of form could not hold itself up. I cannot put it into words, but if I could, it would go something like this: Jeff, after another day of walking aimlessly through Oxford, another day of absolutely nothing, another day of detachment from the world, collapsed on the grass in Christ Church Meadow, totally exhausted, and looked up at a shaft of sunlight coming through the branches of a tree. And Life said:

"LIVE, DAMN IT, LIVE!"

The emptiness collapsed into the form. The form collapsed into the emptiness. And then there was neither form nor emptiness. There was just *this*, with no way of knowing anymore what *this* is. The person dissolved into wonder.

Trees were once again trees. Mountains were once again mountains. Rivers were once again rivers. Starbucks was once again Starbucks. Everything fell back into its rightful place. A chair was allowed to be a chair again, whilst at the same time, of course, it was the divine expression, it was Oneness playing the game of being a chair. A cup of coffee could be a cup of coffee. A thought could be a thought. A sensation could be a sensation. Sadness could be sadness. Love could be love. Everything was itself, and nothing was mine. And because nothing was mine, everything was mine. Words didn't capture it at all. But at last, an ordinary life could be lived. And that ordinary life was the only miracle.

There was a plunge back into the world, *even though* it was only an apparent world, *even though* it was all a dream, *even though* there was no 'me', and no 'others'. Suddenly, after years of being detached and wanting to be detached, there was a relaxation into *what is*. The whole thing collapsed back into a very ordinary life.

But the seeking was dead. The seeker was dead. Jeff died and 'Jeff' was reborn. It was the crucifixion and resurrection all in one, although ultimately nobody was crucified and nobody was resurrected – and that is the ultimate message of the cross.

What is was seen to be the miracle. And it was always enough. The very idea of 'spirituality' went out the window. That concept was no longer needed. Concepts of 'awakening' and 'enlightenment' and 'nothingness' went out the window. Concepts of practices and goals and future attainments went out the window. Why? Because the grass was enough. The tree was enough. The ground beneath my feet was enough. I fell in love with solid ground, or solid ground fell in love with itself, and the seeking of a lifetime was at an end.

As Ramana Maharshi said:

> *The world is illusory.*
> *Brahman alone is real.*
> *Brahman is the world.*

Brahman was the world, and it was all over.

Or, as Zen master Joho exclaimed:

> *Fathomed at last!*
> *Ocean's dried. Void burst.*
> *Without an obstacle in sight,*

It's everywhere!

* * *

When I say "This is it" or "Liberation is not something that you can get", it is not meant as a teaching. It is an attempt to *share* this seeing. I am not a teacher, I could never see myself as that, because there is no longer any reference point here. I have no way of knowing who I am, because it is not possible to separate myself from myself, look back at myself and say what that is. Because I am nothing, I am neither teacher nor student. I am whatever you say I am. And so I am everything too. Call me teacher, call me friend, or call me nothing at all. You are what I am, and I am what you are. And it all ends there, in an intimacy that's beyond words.

"There is nothing to get." It is not a teaching. It is a *confession*.

What is seen here – and I can only ever speak about what is seen here – is that there is nothing to get, because *this* is the miracle. And there is always the possibility that what is being pointed to by those words will be heard. That resonance, that recognition is possible. Perhaps that's why the sharing happens. I don't know.

No, I cannot see myself as a teacher. I just offer the words in my books and meetings and nothing more. I just sing my song. The bird tweets, the cat miaows, and this mind-body organism, or whatever the hell it is, sometimes blabs on about nonduality. And then it goes home and has a cup of tea.

* * *

When you are talking about nonduality, you are always talking about something that cannot be spoken of. If I say "This is already complete and there is nothing to get", I get accused of falling into the absolute. If I say "There is a practice, there is something you can do to get closer to this", I get accused by the nonduality fundamentalists – those who have turned nonduality into their religion, the 'religion of no practice' – of falling into the relative. The Buddha himself said:

> Discard not only conceptions of one's own selfhood and other selves... but also... all ideas about the non-existence of such conceptions.

When we cling to ideas of self, or ideas of no-self, or ideas of practice, or ideas of no-practice, we are falling into duality. After falling into this and so many other conceptual traps over my years as a seeker, what is now seen in absolute clarity is that nonduality cannot be contained by any concept, by any philosophy, by any system, not even the oldest and most refined ones.

The mind always wants to find a place to rest. It wants to come to rest on "There is no self" or "There is no choice". But nonduality offers no home for the homeless. It is a freefall into not-knowing.

You see, there used to be a ferocious, violent intellect here, a mind that could never rest until it had exhausted every possibility, every possible permutation of thought. It would settle for nothing less than absolute freedom. Over the years, so many traps were seen through. So many heavy thought structures were shattered from their very foundations, and seen to be made of nothing but light. My goodness, there were so many traps, so many subtle ways in which I was kidding myself. There are so many ways in which the mind can settle on a concept, on a thought structure, on a belief system, and at the same time—and this is how ingenious it is—proclaim freedom from all concepts and beliefs. The ego can find a million different ways of making it seem like there is no ego.

"I'm free from ego! Me, me, I'm free from ego!"
Yeah, right.

And so these days, when I say "There is nothing you can do to get this", what is also seen is that the moment that pointer turns into a belief, it is no longer true. That is why the guy who really and truly believes "There is nothing you can do, everything is futile!" and so stays in bed all day long, has not been *listening*. The pointers have become concepts for him, they have hardened into beliefs, and led to stagnation and depression. This is such a common trap. I know, I've been there.

There are people out there who truly *believe* that there is no person, no self. They truly *believe* that there is nothing to get. They truly *believe* that there is no future, no Africa, no planet Earth. The belief is the problem. Once it's turned into a belief, it's stagnated. It's a person with a belief. It's my belief versus your belief. And there's no end to it.

In the clear seeing that there is nothing to do—because *this* is already complete—stagnation goes out the window. What I find is that there can be a springing out of bed, the heart fully open to another day of not knowing. "Nothing to do"—just a concept. "Something to do"—another concept.

Nagarjuna said:

To say 'it is' is to grasp for permanence.
To say 'it is not' is to grasp at nihilism.
Therefore a wise person
Does not say 'it is' or 'it is not'.

And Bodhidharma:

Whoever knows that the mind is a fiction and devoid of
anything real knows that his own mind neither exists nor
doesn't exist. Mortals keep creating the mind, claiming it
exists. And Immortals keep negating the mind, claiming it
doesn't exist.

Mind exists, mind doesn't exist. Nothing to do, something to do. Practice, no practice. Past, no past. Self, no self. No need to stick to either polarity, or even negate both polarities. It happens so often: people go to see nonduality teachers or non-teachers and hear that there is nothing they can do to reach liberation, so they give up and get very depressed.

But look: part of the dance is that on this astonishing planet there are a million things to do, or so it would seem! This world – as every child knows – is an adventure playground. It neither exists nor doesn't exist, but either way it's a play.

And so the whole thing ends in the absolute paradox of it all. Nothing to do, lots to do. Nothing, something. Self, no self. There is nobody, there is somebody. The opposites collapse into each other, and what is seen is that *nonduality could never be understood*. Run a million miles from anyone who claims to understand this! This is a plunge into the mystery, totally beyond words. That is what all the words in all the books are really pointing to.

And then, far from being depressing, words such as "This is it" and "There is no path" are all seen to be pointing to this liberation, this unconditional love. And it's seen that they always *have been* pointing to that—we just couldn't see it at the time. Yes, there is nothing to get, because it's all *here*. The intimacy and unconditional love that was always sought are seen to be right *here*.

Until then, yes there is the danger that the words in this book could be taken the wrong way ("You're saying that it's all Oneness, so murder must also be Oneness, so I could just go and kill someone and that's okay because it's all Oneness, right?"). Yes, there is that danger, but there is also this possibility: that what is being communicated will be heard, really heard.

And then the whole duality/nonduality paradox is resolved, and it is seen that there never was a paradox in the first place. The seeing is that Oneness manifests itself as apparently separate beings. Things go on appearing to be separate, whilst at the same time they are all manifestations of the whole. It's the divine dance, it's the cosmic entertainment, it's Lila, it's nothing being everything. And yes, that could all remain on a purely intellectual level. But what is being pointed to here is the seeing—not just intellectual understanding—of this in clarity, and in that seeing, all questions dissolve and what is left, you have no way of knowing.

Yes, it all ends in the mystery, in absolute love. How can I communicate to you the intimacy and freedom and peace and emptiness and fullness of just sitting on a chair, right now? Of just breathing, just sounds happening? The *isness* of this will never be spoken of, and yet it continues to shine, moment by moment, although there are no separate moments at all.

And so the paradox is resolved here, in the absolute simplicity and wonder of what is. In breathing happening, in noises in the room, in the warmth of my mug of tea, in the crunch of the biscuits, in the crumbs falling onto my trousers. The search of a lifetime ends here, and there is only gratitude for the mug of tea, for the biscuits, for this, as it is. Nobody drinks the tea, nobody eats the biscuits, and nobody is writing these words, but still, what a miracle it all is, and how crazy, and innocent in my craziness, I was for all those years, looking for something more than this, when everything I ever needed was right here. Right here, in the place where I am not.

this...

I am caring for a man with terminal
cancer. The disease has spread to his
prostate and testicles, which are now
the size of tennis balls. He is losing
control of his bowels, and in the night
he defecated himself. We laugh and chat
about last night's football match as I
wash faeces off his giant testicles. I
don't tell him there is no suffering, I
don't say "I'm liberated and you're not", I
don't even mention nonduality, I just wash
his testicles. This is it, too.

In a hospice, I hold a woman's hand.
She is dying. Her face is yellow, her
breathing shallow. The stench of urine
and chlorine wafts over a bowl of instant
tomato soup which she hasn't touched. I
am watching myself die. We die together,
in this lonely hospice room with instant
tomato soup and plastic flowers. This is
it, too, and she is the most beautiful
thing I've ever seen.

Now I lie in a hospital bed. A surgeon
has just removed a chunk of flesh from
around my anus. A nurse is shoving gauze
into the open and inflamed wound. It
feels like I'm being stabbed in the anus
and the knife is being twisted around
repeatedly. I ask for some more morphine

but she says I've already had too much.
The pain is all that's happening in the
universe.

A music video blares on the TV next to
my bed. And then suddenly the pain is
gone, and Britney Spears fills all space.
Britney Spears is all that's happening
and the pain is obliterated by a song
called *Womanizer*. It's like the pain never
happened. If it happened, it happened
a billion years ago. If it happened, it
happened to someone else.

And then suddenly the stabbing pain
arises again. I didn't know such pain was
possible. There are tears in my eyes. I
nearly pass out. And then more Britney.
*"Womanizer, woman-womanizer, you're a
womanizer, oh womanizer, oh you're a
womanizer, baby."* The pain is absorbed
into Britney's dance routine.

There is no consistency here. Nothing is
carried over from one moment to the next.
There is only the rawness of experiencing.
Stab, Britney, stab, Britney. The universe
breathes in and out.

8

An Extraordinary Absence

It is accomplished.

– John 19:30

Life is a singular movement. Sometimes loud, sometimes violent, sometimes ferocious. Sometimes sweet, sometimes soft, sometimes as gentle as a feather. Sometimes life roars, sometimes it whispers, but it always moves. And yet at the heart of that movement, there is no origin, no point of reference, no centre; no 'heart' at all, if truth be told. And truth can never be told.

Words such as these attempt to tell the truth that cannot be told, and yet the words themselves are but another part of that infinite movement, that inexpressible aliveness that fuels all things, moves all things, *is* all things in their totality. Life is a movement, and its origin is movement. Its origin is itself.

Life has no centre because it has no circumference. There's nowhere where it ends, nowhere where it begins. It is simply a spontaneous expression of aliveness, happening now, now and now, leaving no trace of itself, projecting nothing into the future, concealing nothing, giving itself totally and completely and exhausting itself in that expression, leaving no residue. It is all things, and yet it is no thing.

Life – or what we call 'life', anyway – is totally beyond mind, too alive for mind, too free for mind, too *total* for it, and that total and complete expression, which we are in no way separate from, happens constantly. Life throws itself out of itself again and again to create the illusion of a world, to give us this wonderful dream of waking life. And yet of course, life does nothing at all. There are no separate events, people, places, and so nothing separate from anything else has ever been done. From the Big Bang, and from before that, there has only been one happening, and it is happening now. No happening separate from any other happening, although the illusion is a good one. And the illusion is what we might call 'me'.

* * *

I'm standing near the sea not far from Brighton Marina. A storm rages. The wind nearly knocks me off my feet. Waves crash onto a jetty. The roar is deafening. Seagulls struggle to fly in the gale.

And yet the wind is not separate from me. The sea, the jetty, the seagulls are not separate from what I am. In fact, I cannot even say that. All I can say is that, presently, life, Oneness, aliveness, Being – call it what you want – appears as the sea, the jetty, the wind, the seagulls, and this body as it stands there in the gale. It is all a present appearance, appearing for no-one. It exists only to be itself, and for no other reason. Nothing exists apart from it; nothing that could ever be known, anyway. This is how the Source appears now. This is the movie playing out presently. This is the dream, and it is total, and it is complete, and it needs nothing else. Life has already accomplished what it set out to do.

I am one with it, I am separate from it, I am something, I am nothing, I see it, it is seen by no-one. All just words. Life needs no more words. Its words are already the crashing of the waves against the beach, the foam building up along the shore, the screech of the seagulls, the deafening roar of the wind blasting my eardrums. Its words are already being spoken, and life doesn't need anyone to speak for it, especially not me. The words of life are being shouted, screamed. They deafen me. I am annihilated by them.

And not just here, in this storm, but everywhere, all the time. In the quietest moments, and in the loudest moments, life speaks. And the quiet moments and loud moments are both perfect expressions. It's all One Taste, all the taste of life itself, living itself as it must. 'Jeff' is just a relic from the past. 'Jeff' is a fossil. Who needs the past? Where has it gone, anyway? Who needs the future? It never arrives, anyway. Nothing can begin to touch the wonder of this. Of this moment, this present expression of life.

Like newborn babies, we always see it for the first time. The sea roars for the first time. The seagull screeches for the first time. Back inside my room, where it's warm and cosy, I sip a cup of tea for the first time. Nobody could tell me otherwise.

This needs no defending. It does not need to be proved, to be argued. It is its own defence, it is its own proof. Nobody can argue with the *isness*. Well, they can actually. And they do. And that's the misery of a lifetime.

But when that argument ends, *what is* is always enough. More than enough.

* * *

Life is an offering, and it offers itself now, now and now.

197

It offers present sights, sounds, smells and feelings and asks nothing of you. And yet we spend our lives wanting so much more. Well, that is our misery. In the absence of that, there is only *this*, as there always has been. Only ever what presents itself now. Only what emerges presently from the Source, only what manifests out of the Unknown; *you get only that and nothing more.*

And right there, it is all released. The burden of a lifetime, gone in the blink of an eye. This 'Jeff' character who suffered and suffered, and sought a way out of his suffering, where is he? He's simply not there. Who is writing these words then? Is Jeff writing these words, you may ask? There is only that question. No answer rises up to meet it, and so the question dies away, dissolving back into the Source.

This liberation, it has nothing at all to do with you. If you think that 'you' can reach liberation, you'll be chasing your own tail for the rest of your life. You cannot reach liberation, you cannot awaken, because *this* is already fully awake. Already whole, already complete, and it's only in the dream of separation that the search appears to have any validity at all. But in the falling away of the seeking, the miracle is revealed. And the miracle is life itself, and life itself has *always* been the miracle. We just couldn't see it, because we were too busy trying to be someone, trying to become something, trying to be good, trying to understand, trying to succeed, or even trying not to try.

But in the clear seeing of this miracle, all of that is rendered obsolete. In the seeing that there is only *this*, in the shockingly simple and simply shocking waking up from the dream of separation, there is a death, and that death, as Jesus said, is the only salvation. You have to lose your life to save it. And so when there is no-one, there isn't an empty void, a lonely and joyless black space devoid of all qualities, no, no, no. That void is *full*, it is bursting with life. With the sea roaring, and seagulls screeching, and the wind crashing against your face, and a steaming mug of tea, and... *life, damn it, life!* The emptiness is fullness, the void is fully alive, the nothingness is life in all its magnificence, and that is the freedom that the so-called 'individual' could never, ever find.

And in that, all the concepts in the world dissolve. They are seen to be what they always were: words, just words. And beyond those words, the foam from the crashing waves fascinates me more than anything in the world, and those seagulls are as precious as my very own children, and the wind is simply life caressing me, and there is a fragile beauty here that words could never touch at all. It's a wordless, bitter-sweet, tender love affair with life, a life that's given now, freely, to be seen, just to be seen.

This liberation, this love, this tenderness, this innocence will never be put into words, never communicated, never captured, and yet it is all there is, forever appearing everywhere, always being everything, always rejecting nothing, embracing you–or what you take yourself to be–in every single damn moment.

Life itself is the only miracle. There is no other. An extraordinary absence is a perfect presence, nothing is everything, and in that, everything is resolved.

All doctrines split asunder,
Zen teaching cast away —
Fourscore years and one.
The sky now cracks and falls,
The earth cleaves open —
In the heart of fire
Lies a hidden spring.

- Giun

Visit Jeff Foster's website:

www.lifewithoutacentre.com

NON-DUALITY PRESS

If you enjoyed this book, you might be interested in these related titles published by Non-Duality Press.

CONSCIOUS.TV

CONSCIOUS.TV is a TV channel broadcasting on the Internet at www.conscious.tv. Certain programmes are also broadcast on Satellite TV stations based in the UK. The channel aims to stimulate debate, question, enquire, inform, enlighten, encourage and inspire people in the areas of Consciousness, Healing and Psychology.

There are already over 100 interviews to watch including several with communicators on Non-Duality including Gangaji, Jeff Foster, Catherine Noyce, Richard Lang, Roger Linden, Tony Parsons, Halina Pytlasinska, Genpo Roshi, Richard Sylvester, Rupert Spira, Florian Schlosser, Francis Lucille, and Pamela Wilson. Some of these interviewees also have books available from Non-Duality Press.

Do check out the channel as we are interested in your feedback and any ideas you may have for future programmes. Email us at info@conscious.tv with your ideas or if you would like to be on our email newsletter list.

WWW.CONSCIOUS.TV

CONSCIOUS.TV and *NON-DUALITY PRESS*
present two unique DVD releases

CONVERSATIONS ON NON-DUALITY – VOLUME 1

Tony Parsons – *The Open Secret* • Rupert Spira –
The Transparency of Things – Parts 1 & 2 • Richard Lang –
Seeing Who You Really Are

CONVERSATIONS ON NON-DUALITY – VOLUME 2

Jeff Foster – *Life Without a Centre* • Richard Sylvester –
I Hope You Die Soon • Roger Linden – *The Elusive Obvious*

Available to order from: www.non-dualitypress.com

CPSIA information can be obtained at www.ICGtesting.com
226839LV00001B/99/P